The CHEW

An Essential Guide to Cooking and Entertaining

ALSO AVAILABLE FROM *THE CHEW*

The *New York Times* best-selling books:
The Chew: Food. Life. Fun.
The Chew: What's for Dinner?
The Chew: A Year of Celebrations

The CHEW

An Essential Guide to Cooking and Entertaining

RECIPES, WIT, AND WISDOM FROM THE CHEW HOSTS

Edited by Ashley Archer

KINGSWELL

S ANGELES • NEW YORK

PAGE 2: **Michael Symon's Greek Lamb Wellington, recipe on page 184.**

PAGE 6: **Carla Hall's Cheesy Pull-Apart Pesto Bread, recipe on page 168.**

Content coordinator: Taylor Goode
Researchers: Janet Arvelo and Kerry McConnell
Food Photographer: Andrew Scrivani
Senior Food Stylist: Jackie Rothong
Food Stylists: Ian McNulty, Alexandra Utter
Assistant Food Stylist: Kelly Janke
Prop stylist: Francine Matalon-Degni

Cover cast photographer: ABC/Craig Sjodin

For information address Kingswell, 1101 Flower Street, Glendale, California 91201

Editorial Director: Wendy Lefkon
Executive Editor: Laura Hopper
Designer: Gregory Wakabayashi / Welcome Enterprises, Inc., New York

ISBN 978-1-4847-5355-2
FAC-008598-16050

Printed in the United States of America
FIRST PAPERBACK EDITION, APRIL 2016
10 9 8 7 6 5 4 3 2 1

SUSTAINABLE FORESTRY INITIATIVE

Certified Chain of Custody
At Least 20% Certified Forest Content
www.sfiprogram.org
SFI-00993

For Text Only

CONTENTS

ENJOY OUR NEW FEATURE!

MANY RECIPES ARE DESIGNATED AS ONE OF THE FOLLOWING:

MAKE AHEAD   SLOW COOKER SWAP   ON THE LIGHTER SIDE   TIME-SAVER

The Chew: An Essential Guide to Cooking and Entertaining

INTRODUCTION

After five fabulous years of making *The Chew* and cooking nearly 4,000 recipes, we understand choosing the right meal can become a little overwhelming. With this book, we decided to make things a little easier for you.

Our hope is that *The Essential Guide to Cooking and Entertaining* offers you, The Chew Family, the absolute essentials to have at hand so you are never caught off guard, whatever the meal, moment, or mishap.

We offer here some of the most popular downloaded dishes we have cooked on the show, a greatest hits album if you will. Literally millions of viewers have voted—and we thought, why not give you what you want?

Michael, Clinton, Carla, Daphne, and Mario have picked some of their favorite recipes over the seasons and included some of their best stories, tips, and tricks, to keep your heart in the kitchen. Whether because of simplicity, memories, or yumminess, these are their all-time winners. From The Chew Family to yours.

Our party in the kitchen every day on ABC is inspired by the feedback we get from viewers who love what we cook. They share with us their own recipes as well as their reaction to ours. It's a delicious loop. Food always was and ever will be an expression of friendship and adventure. We hope you find those two things on our show and in this book. Enjoy.

—Gordon Elliott, Executive Producer

BACK TO

I love to throw dinner parties. There is nothing better than a house filled with good music, great friends, delicious food, and, of course, fabulous cocktails. You know, the secret to becoming successful in the kitchen is really just trial and error . . . seriously! The only way to become a confident cook is to just keep trying things out until you've mastered them. I think with anything you do, practice makes perfect. So, we've pulled together some of our favorite recipes from the show to help you get started. Recipes that we think everyone can and should master. Whether you're a seasoned cook brushing up on your technique or a first-time fryer, there is plenty of inspiration in here to help you put together a fabulous feast!

—CLINTON KELLY

BASICS

Ham and Cheese Danish

Serves: 2–4   **Prep Time: 10 minutes**   **Cook Time: 45 minutes**

I love to make this dish for my husband, John, on the weekends because it feels just **a little bit fancy**, like something we might have eaten in Paris on our honeymoon. It's so easy to put together and a great make-ahead brunch dish. I like to change up the filling from time to time; spinach and cheddar work well, and even chocolate hazelnut spread with bananas or strawberry jam as a special treat for the kids.

2 tablespoons olive oil

1 onion, thinly sliced

Salt and freshly ground black pepper, to taste

1 sheet store-bought puff pastry, thawed

¼ cup Gruyère cheese, shredded

4 slices cooked ham

1 large egg

¼ cup crème fraîche

2 tablespoons chives, finely chopped

1. Preheat oven to 400°F.

2. In a medium sauté pan over medium low heat, add 2 tablespoons olive oil. Add sliced onions and cook until golden brown, about 20–30 minutes. Season with salt and pepper, and cool to room temperature.

3. To form the Danish, begin with the long edge of the pastry on the bottom of your work surface. On the right half of the pastry, place half of the caramelized onions, half of the cheese, and half of the ham, leaving a 1-inch border around the edges. Repeat with remaining ingredients, seasoning each layer with salt and pepper.

4. In a small bowl, beat one egg. Brush the 1-inch border with the beaten egg, then carefully fold the pastry over the ingredients like you're closing a book. Crimp the edges all around the border with a fork to seal and transfer the pastry to a parchment lined sheet pan. Brush the entire pastry with the remaining beaten egg. Using a sharp knife, cut 3 or 4 1-inch slits in the top of the pastry. Bake for 25 minutes or until golden brown.

5. Let the pastry sit for about 5 minutes and serve with crème fraîche and chopped chives.

CARLA'S "MAKE AHEAD" TIP
Fill and seal the pastry and then pop in the freezer. When you're ready to bake, just brush with the egg and put straight into the oven. You don't even need to defrost!

Omelette in a Jar

Serves: 1   Prep Time: 1 minute   **Cook Time:** 3 minutes

If you're like me, you wake up in the morning hungry for something delicious. I love omelettes for breakfast and there are so many different flavor combinations that I never get tired of eating them. What's exhausting, though, is the cleanup! When I discovered that I could make an omelette in less than 2 minutes in the microwave and with no mess, **my mind was blown!**

Nonstick cooking spray

1 tablespoon milk or cream

¼ cup of torn spinach

2 tablespoons shredded cheddar cheese

1–2 tablespoons chopped ham or smoked turkey

2 eggs

Salt and freshly ground black pepper, to taste

1. Spray a 16-ounce, microwave-safe glass jar with nonstick cooking spray. Add the milk, spinach, cheese, and ham to the jar. (You can do this part the night before.)

2. Crack the two eggs into the jar. Season with salt and pepper, then place the lid back on and shake vigorously for 20–30 seconds, until the eggs are pale yellow. Remove the lid and microwave for 90 seconds.

3. Carefully remove from the microwave and check for doneness. Return to the microwave for 15–30 seconds to finish cooking as needed.

4. Remove to a plate or eat warm, right from the jar.

Lemon-Ricotta Pancakes

Serves: 4   Prep Time: *5 minutes*   **Cook Time:** *15 minutes*

I came up with this recipe for a segment we do on the show called "Use It Up," where I teach *The Chew* viewers how to use up the last bits from their bags of chips, loaves of bread, or jars of peanut butter. This one was for lemon curd, and let me tell you, **these pancakes were so good** that I had to pry them out of Carla's hands for a crumb! You know that lady loves a pucker.

Leftover lemon curd, about 2–3 tablespoons

1 cup whole milk

2 eggs

2 tablespoons sugar

1 teaspoon vanilla extract

1 cup fresh ricotta

1 cup all-purpose flour

½ teaspoon baking powder

½ teaspoon baking soda

Pinch of salt

Butter for the pan

Powdered sugar, to garnish

Whipped cream, optional

1. Open the leftover jar of lemon curd. Microwave for 20 seconds with the lid off. Add ¼ cup of the milk to the jar, return lid, and shake vigorously. Pour the lemon curd mixture into a medium bowl and whisk in the remaining milk, eggs, sugar, vanilla, and ricotta and set aside.

2. Add the dry ingredients to another large bowl and whisk to combine, then stir in the ricotta mixture.

3. Preheat a skillet over medium heat. Melt the butter into the pan. Pour batter into the hot pan. Cook the pancakes for about 3 or 4 minutes, until the undersides are golden-brown and a few bubbles begin to form on top. Flip the pancakes and cook until golden-brown, about 3 more minutes. Repeat with the remaining batter. Garnish with powdered sugar and whipped cream if you've got it.

Clinton and Jessie Palmer get ready for the big game.

The Chew: An Essential Guide to Cooking and Entertaining

Oven-Roasted BLT with Tangy Mayo

Serves: 2   Prep Time: 15 minutes   Cook Time: 2 hours, 30 minutes

What's better in the summer than a BLT with crispy bacon, a nice ripe, juicy tomato, and crunchy lettuce? I say nothing. **It's simple and fulfilling.** When I get a hankering for this classic sandwich the rest of the year—when tomatoes are not in season—I turn to the oven for help. The addition of thyme and black pepper really brings out the sweetness of the tomatoes.

FOR THE OVEN-DRIED TOMATOES:

1 pound vine-ripened (or beef steak) tomatoes, sliced ¼-inch thick

3 tablespoons olive oil, plus more for brushing

Salt and freshly ground black pepper, to taste

1 tablespoon fresh thyme leaves

FOR THE TANGY MAYO:

2 large egg yolks

2 tablespoons water

1 tablespoon distilled white vinegar

1 tablespoon cider vinegar

¾ teaspoon salt

1½ cups canola oil

FOR THE BLTS:

½ pound double-thick bacon, about 8 slices

4 slices Pullman or sourdough bread, sliced ¼-inch thick and toasted

2 tablespoons Dijon mustard

4 tablespoons tangy mayo

4 to 6 oven-dried tomatoes

½ red onion, thinly sliced

12–16 fresh basil leaves

FOR THE OVEN-DRIED TOMATOES:

1. Preheat oven to 300°F.

2. Place a roasting rack over a sheet tray and brush with olive oil. Lay the tomato slices out on the roasting rack, then drizzle with olive oil. Season with salt and pepper, and sprinkle with the thyme leaves. Bake until caramelized, about 2 to 2½ hours.

FOR THE TANGY MAYO:

3. In the bowl of a food processor, add the egg yolks, water, vinegars, and salt. Puree until combined, then pour in the oil in a thin stream while the processor is running. Store in the refrigerator in an airtight container.

FOR THE BLTs:

4. Lay the bacon out in an even layer on a cold, nonstick sauté pan and place over medium heat. Cook until crisp and then drain on a paper towel–lined plate.

5. Spread one piece of bread with 1 tablespoon of Dijon mustard and the other piece with a thick layer of the tangy mayo. Top one slice of the bread with the bacon, oven-dried tomatoes, shaved red onion, and basil leaves. Top with the remaining piece of bread.

6. Repeat with the remaining ingredients to make another sandwich then slice diagonally and serve.

MICHAEL'S "ENTERTAINING" TIP
If you have any leftover roasted tomatoes, just place them in a jar, top them with olive oil, and pop in the fridge. They make a great appetizer spooned over a grilled or toasted baguette spread with ricotta cheese.

Glazed Corned Beef and Cabbage on Rye

Serves: 12   Prep Time: 30 minutes   Cook Time: 3 hours, 30 minutes

In New York City, there is a great delicatessen or two in almost any neighborhood in the city. So I'm lucky that I get to eat these sandwiches, piled high with tons of meat and slathered with tangy mustard, anytime I want. If you're living in the rest of the country, I developed this **super-easy recipe** that I think you'll love.

3 pounds corned beef

½ cup honey mustard

2 tablespoons light brown sugar

½ cup cider vinegar

1 tablespoon granulated sugar

¼ cup olive oil

½ head green cabbage, thinly sliced

1 red onion, thinly sliced

¼ cup parsley, chopped

1 tablespoon caraway seeds, toasted

Salt and freshly ground black pepper, to taste

2 loaves rye bread, toasted

1. Preheat oven to 350°F.

2. Place the corned beef in a 9x13 baking dish. In a small bowl, combine the honey mustard and brown sugar. Brush the fatty side of the corned beef with half of the honey mustard mixture. Pour enough water into the baking dish so that it covers about 1 inch of the beef. Cover the baking dish with aluminum foil and bake for 3 hours. Uncover and brush the corned beef with the rest of the honey mustard mixture. Bake uncovered for 30 minutes more. You can do this a day or two in advance and just reheat in a low oven.

3. Meanwhile, add the vinegar, granulated sugar, and olive oil to a large bowl and whisk to combine. Add the cabbage, onion, parsley, and caraway seeds. Toss to coat and season with salt and pepper. Set aside.

4. Remove meat to a platter and let rest for 10 minutes. Cut the corned beef on a diagonal, against the grain, into ½-inch slices.

TO BUILD THE SANDWICH:

5. Slather some honey mustard on one side of 2 pieces of bread. Top one piece of toast with a few slices of corned beef. Top with the cabbage slaw. Top the sandwich with the second piece of toast, mustard-side down. Repeat with remaining ingredients.

Pan-Fried Dumpling

Serves: 8   **Prep Time:** *10 minutes*   **Cook Time:** *5 minutes*

This is **an oldie but goodie** from way back in my catering days. I used to make hundreds of these little babies and freeze them. Then when it was time to party, I'd just put them straight into the sauté pan with a little bit of vegetable oil, add some water to steam, and boom, you've got yourself an appetizer that's perfect for any occasion.

FOR THE DUMPLING:

1½ pounds ground chicken, white and dark meat mixed

1 egg yolk

2 garlic cloves, minced

3 scallions, sliced, plus more to garnish

1 tablespoon grated fresh ginger

2 tablespoons low-sodium soy sauce

2 teaspoons fish sauce, optional

1 package square wonton wrappers

2 tablespoons vegetable oil

FOR THE DIPPING SAUCE:

¼ cup low-sodium soy sauce

2 teaspoons Worcestershire sauce

1 teaspoon freshly grated ginger

1 teaspoon chili paste

FOR THE DUMPLING:

1. Combine the first seven ingredients in a large bowl and stir until thoroughly combined. Scoop out a small tablespoon of the mixture and place in the center of a wonton wrapper. Dampen the edges of the wrapper with water and bring the four corners up to meet. Press the edges together to seal the dumpling. Repeat with remaining filling and wrappers. This can be done up to a month in advance and stored in the freezer.

2. Heat a large nonstick skillet over medium-high heat with a thin layer of vegetable oil until hot. Add the wontons in batches and cook until golden on the bottom, about 2 minutes. Add 2 tablespoons of water to the pan and cover with a lid. Steam for 3 minutes. Remove to a paper towel–lined plate and cool slightly before serving with the dipping sauce.

FOR THE DIPPING SAUCE:

3. Mix the ingredients together in a small bowl and serve with dumplings.

DAPHNE'S "FREEZER" TIP
Make a huge batch of these and divide them into two-person servings and freeze. That way you can cook for two or ten without having to thaw the entire batch.

Penne alla Vodka

Serves: 6   **Prep Time:** 2 minutes   **Cook Time:** 15 minutes

It's unclear how this dish originated, but it is definitely Italian and **undeniably delicious!** I know it seems a little strange adding Russian vodka to Italian pasta, but when the alcohol cooks down into the sauce it adds a rich, almost spicy flavor that goes perfectly with the sweetness of the tomato paste and saltiness of the bacon. I'm guessing that you already have all of the ingredients to make this dish in your kitchen right now . . . so get cooking!

1 pound penne pasta

Kosher salt

6 slices bacon, chopped

2 cloves garlic, thinly sliced

¼ cup tomato paste

¼ cup vodka

½ cup heavy cream

Pinch of nutmeg

2–3 tablespoons Parmesan, for garnish

1. Bring a large pot of salted water to a boil and cook the penne 1 minute short of the package instructions. Drain, reserving some pasta water for sauce.

2. In a large sauté pan, cook bacon over medium heat until crisp, about 6–8 minutes. Add the garlic and tomato paste and cook until garlic is fragrant and tomato paste begins to caramelize, about 3 minutes more.

3. Stir in the vodka and allow sauce to reduce by half. Add the cream and season with nutmeg and salt to taste. Adjust thickness of sauce with pasta water as needed.

4. Add cooked penne and some reserved pasta water and toss to coat.

5. Serve with a generous sprinkling of Parmesan.

Chicken Paillard with Grilled Pineapple Salad

When the weather starts to get warm and it's time to dust off those grills, I turn to this super fresh summer dish. There is such sweetness from the grilled pineapple, plus a little bitterness from the radicchio, and with that tang from the lemon, **you'll get a dish packed with flavor.** What I love about this, too, is that it's really healthy, but it doesn't feel like diet food.

4 boneless skinless chicken breasts, pounded to ¼-inch thickness

Salt and freshly ground black pepper, to taste

¼ cup olive oil

1 pineapple peeled, cored, and cut into spears

FOR THE VINAIGRETTE:

2 tablespoons freshly squeezed lemon juice

1 tablespoon chopped parsley

2 teaspoons Dijon mustard

Olive oil

Salt and freshly ground black pepper, to taste

2 heads radicchio, outer leaves and core removed, cut in half lengthwise, sliced into ½-inch strips

1 cup julienned carrots

2 tablespoons torn mint leaves

1. Preheat a grill or grill pan to medium heat.

2. Season the chicken with salt and pepper and drizzle with olive oil. Place the chicken on the grill pan and cook for about 3–4 minutes per side, until cooked through. Serve with the pineapple salad.

FOR THE PINEAPPLE SALAD:

3. Place the pineapple spears on the grill (or grill pan) and cook for 2–3 minutes per side, or until caramelized. Remove from the grill and cut into bite-size pieces.

4. Meanwhile, make a vinaigrette by whisking together the lemon juice, parsley, Dijon mustard, and a drizzle of olive oil in a large mixing bowl. Season with salt and pepper. Add the grilled and chopped pineapple, radicchio, carrots, and mint to the bowl. Toss until coated in the vinaigrette. Serve on top of or alongside the chicken cutlets.

DAPHNE'S "PINEAPPLE" TIP
I have a great tip for getting the sweetest pineapple possible on your dinner table. Twist off the leaves in a clockwise motion and turn your pineapple upside down and let it sit for about 30 minutes before you cut into it. Doing this allows the juices and sugars to redistribute throughout the pineapple, making every bite the perfect bite.

Chicken Mole Enchiladas

This dish is **great for beginners** because it's likely that you have all of the ingredients you need to make these enchiladas already in your pantry. Traditional moles can take hours or even days to make, but this one comes together in just around an hour. In fact, you could make this tonight, and *holy mole* it is amazing!

1 onion, roughly chopped

3 cloves garlic, peeled

1 jalapeño, seeded

2 tablespoons vegetable oil

Salt and freshly ground black pepper, to taste

2 ounces unsweetened chocolate, chopped

½ cup brewed coffee

¼ cup raisins

1 tablespoon chili powder

½ teaspoon cinnamon

1 tablespoon ground cumin

2 tablespoons dark brown sugar

½ cup toasted peanuts

1 cup chicken broth

1 cup tomato sauce

Juice of half an orange

1 12-ounce dark beer

2 cups cooked shredded chicken

2 cups Monterey Jack cheese, shredded

10 corn tortillas

¼ cup sour cream

FOR THE GARNISH:

3 scallions, sliced for garnish

1 avocado, pitted and diced

1 white onion, chopped

2 tablespoons cilantro, chopped

1. Preheat oven to 400°F.

2. Toss onion, garlic, and jalapeño with vegetable oil, salt, and pepper and place on a sheet pan. Roast 10–15 minutes, until vegetables have browned and are soft but not mushy. In a small bowl, add chopped chocolate and pour hot coffee over to melt. Stir to combine.

3. To the carafe of a blender, add the roasted vegetables, chocolate mixture, raisins, chili powder, cinnamon, cumzain, dark brown sugar, peanuts, chicken broth, tomato sauce, orange juice, and beer. Blend until very smooth, then transfer to a saucepan. Cook the sauce over medium-high heat for about 15 minutes. In a large bowl, add the shredded chicken, 1 cup shredded cheese, and 1 cup of mole.

TO ASSEMBLE:

4. Place tortillas in a resealable bag and microwave on high for 20 seconds to make the tortillas warm and pliable. In the bottom of a 9x13 baking dish, ladle about 1 cup of the sauce to coat the bottom of the dish. Place one tortilla on a plate and fill with a generous amount of chicken filling and roll up. Place enchilada seam-side down in a 9x13 baking dish. Repeat with remaining tortillas and filling. Top with remaining sauce and cheese. Bake 30 minutes.

5. Top with sour cream, scallions, avocado, white onion, and cilantro.

Slow-Roasted Salmon with Avocado Salad

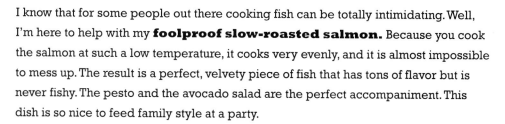

Serves: 6–8   Prep Time: 20–25 minutes   Cook Time: 45–50 minutes

I know that for some people out there cooking fish can be totally intimidating. Well, I'm here to help with my **foolproof slow-roasted salmon.** Because you cook the salmon at such a low temperature, it cooks very evenly, and it is almost impossible to mess up. The result is a perfect, velvety piece of fish that has tons of flavor but is never fishy. The pesto and the avocado salad are the perfect accompaniment. This dish is so nice to feed family style at a party.

1 tablespoon coriander seeds

¼ cup honey

1 orange, juiced

1 cup water

1 side of salmon, skinned and deboned

2 tablespoons extra virgin olive oil

Salt and freshly ground black pepper, to taste

FOR THE ALMOND BASIL PESTO:

½ cup blanched almonds, lightly toasted

1 bunch basil, leaves torn

2 garlic cloves, peeled

⅓ cup extra virgin olive oil, plus more if needed

Salt and freshly ground black pepper, to taste

FOR THE AVOCADO SALAD:

¼ cup extra virgin olive oil

1 orange, juice and zest

2 tablespoons champagne vinegar

½ shallot, sliced thinly

Salt and freshly ground black pepper, to taste

2 avocados, diced

1 Fresno chili, minced

FOR THE SALMON:

1. Preheat oven to 225°F. Line a baking sheet with a silicon mat or parchment paper.

2. In a small saucepot, toast the coriander seeds until fragrant, about 1 minute. Add the honey, orange juice, water, salt, and pepper. Bring to a boil and reduce to a simmer. Cook for 15 minutes or until thick and reduced by half.

3. Season the salmon with salt, pepper, and a drizzle of olive oil. Transfer to the prepared baking sheet and brush with the honey glaze. Bake for 30–35 minutes for medium rare, slightly opaque in the middle. Cook longer for a more well-done piece of salmon. Remove from the oven and allow to cool slightly. Smear the salmon with the pesto and top with the avocado salad.

FOR THE ALMOND BASIL PESTO:

4. Combine the first three ingredients in a food processor with salt and pepper. Begin to process and slowly drizzle in the oil. Taste to adjust seasoning as needed. The pesto should be thick but spreadable. Process with more oil or more basil to adjust consistency.

FOR THE AVOCADO SALAD:

5. In a medium bowl, whisk together the orange juice and zest, vinegar, shallot, salt, and pepper. Add in the avocado and Fresno chili and toss to coat.

Easy Oven-Roasted Turkey Breast

Serves: 4   Prep Time: 5 minutes   Cook Time: 45–50 minutes

The first time I made this roasted turkey breast, it was for John, Philo, and me on our first Thanksgiving at home, just the three of us. I didn't want to make a whole turkey because there was no way we could ever eat it all, and Philo, being so young, wasn't really into dark meat. Since then, I make it every year because it is so moist and flavorful. And since you're not cooking the whole bird, it's juicy and tender every time; and it only take 45 minutes to roast. **How great is that?**

1 whole turkey breast, bone-in, skin-on, split in half

½ cup butter, softened

2 tablespoons fresh thyme leaves, chopped

2 tablespoons olive oil

Salt and freshly ground black pepper, to taste

¼ cup parsley, roughly chopped

1 tablespoon lemon zest

1 tablespoon Pecorino Romano

1. Preheat oven to 350°F.

2. In a small mixing bowl, combine butter and thyme. Season with salt and pepper and mix until fully combined.

3. Take the compound butter and, using your hands, carefully rub it under and over the skin of the turkey breast. Be careful not to tear the skin. Place the turkey breasts on a baking sheet and drizzle with olive oil. Sprinkle with salt and pepper.

4. Place the baking sheet in the oven and roast for 45 minutes, or until the temperature registers 160°F with a meat thermometer. Remove from oven and allow to rest 10 minutes.

5. Meanwhile, combine parsley, lemon zest, and Pecorino Romano in a small mixing bowl. Drizzle in about a tablespoon of olive oil and season with salt and pepper.

6. To serve, slice the turkey breast and serve with parsley mixture.

Pan-Seared Strip Steak with Mushrooms and Caramelized Onions

Serves: 4   Prep Time: 30 minutes   Cook Time: 10 minutes

This is one of the easiest recipes I know for making a seared steak with pan sauce. A cut of meat like the New York strip **doesn't need a lot of bells and whistles** because it's a cut that has so much flavor; really, you just need to cook it properly, which means that you don't flip it before it's ready. Make sure that you get a nice crust on that meat and only flip it once. The biggest mistake that people make is moving around their meat too much in the pan. Just put the tongs down people!

2 tablespoons olive oil

2 8-ounce strip steaks

Salt and freshly ground black pepper, to taste

3 tablespoons olive oil

¼ pound bacon, sliced ½-inch thick

1 8-ounce container of button mushrooms, sliced ¼-inch thick

½ onion, sliced thinly

2 garlic cloves, finely minced

1 12-ounce can of beer

¼ cup sour cream

¼ cup parsley, leaves

1. Take the strip steaks out of the fridge 30 minutes prior to cooking.

2. Heat a medium-size cast iron pan over medium-high heat and a sauté pan over medium-high heat.

3. Season the steaks generously with salt and pepper and drizzle with olive oil.

4. Put the steaks in the cast-iron pan and cook 3–4 minutes on each side, or until deep golden brown.

5. Take the steaks out of the pan and let rest for at least 10 minutes.

6. In the other sauté pan, add about 3 tablespoons of olive oil and add the bacon. Let crisp for 2–3 minutes.

7. Add the mushrooms and toss to coat. Let brown for another 2–3 minutes. Add the onions and garlic and season everything with salt and pepper. Toss and cook for 1–2 minutes longer, until the onions begin to wilt. Add the can of beer and bring to a simmer. Allow sauce to reduce by half.

8. Turn off the heat, add the sour cream, and stir to emulsify. Replace the pan on the heat and bring back up to a simmer. Taste and adjust for seasoning. Add the parsley, stir to incorporate, and take the pan off the heat. When the steak is rested, slice and plate. Pour the mushroom sauce over the steak and serve.

Beef Bourguignon

Serves: 4   **Prep Time:** *30 minutes*   **Cook Time:** *2 hours, 30 minutes*

When I think of beef bourguignon, **I think of Julia Child.** In fact the first time I tried to make this dish, it was because I had just seen that movie *Julie & Julia* and I thought, I can make that! And really it's not that hard: it just takes a while. I think everyone should know how to make this dish, so I've included this incredibly delicious, classic version for you to try.

1 bay leaf

3 sprigs fresh thyme

3 sprigs parsley

1 tablespoon olive oil

½ small yellow onion, or 1 whole shallot, chopped

¼ pound thick-cut bacon, diced

1½ cups beef stock

1½ pounds stewing beef, cut into 1½-inch cubes

¼ cup all-purpose flour

1¼ cups red wine

½ cup sliced mushrooms

1 cup carrots, chopped

1 cup frozen pearl onions, thawed

1 cup frozen peas, thawed

Salt and freshly ground black pepper, to taste

1. Tie together the bay leaf, thyme, and parsley to make a bouquet garni.

2. In a Dutch oven, heat the olive oil over medium heat and add the onion or shallot and bacon. Cook until slightly browned, and then remove from the pan and reserve, saving the fat in the Dutch oven.

3. Meanwhile, in a small saucepan, heat the stock until just at a simmer. Toss the beef in the flour, add to Dutch oven and brown on all sides.

4. Deglaze the pan with the red wine, scraping the bottom of the pan as you pour.

5. Add the hot stock, bouquet garni, mushrooms, carrots, and reserved bacon and onion. Add pearl onions and peas.

6. Cover and simmer for 2–2½ hours.

7. Season the beef all over with salt and pepper. When the meat is fork tender, spoon the stew into bowls and enjoy.

MICHAEL'S "LEFTOVER" TIP
If by chance you have some of this left over, I recommend that you make little stew pockets out of puff pastry just like Daphne did with Ham and Cheese Danish (p.15). Just make sure that you fill the pockets with chilled stew so you don't melt the pastry.

Cheesy Hasselback Potatoes

Serves: 6–8   **Prep Time:** 15 minutes   **Cook Time:** 45–50 minutes

A viewer once asked me, "What should I do with the leftovers of this dish?" My response? I said I'd give her twenty bucks if "there was a single crumb of this left in the pan at the end of the meal," and I meant it! This cheesy, buttery potato dish is kind of like a casserole, but it's a little bit sexier and a lot more fun to make. **This combination of cheese and potato is legendary!** Originating in the 1940s at the Scandic Hasselbacken in Stockholm, Sweden, these potatoes become crispy and golden brown on the outside while the inside stays fluffy and creamy, like little pillows of happiness!

1 tablespoon butter

4 large russet potatoes, scrubbed clean

1 pound Gruyère, ¼-inch-thick slices, cut into 2-inch squares

Salt and freshly ground black pepper, to taste

1 cup sour cream

1 cup milk

½ teaspoon nutmeg, freshly grated

¼ cup prosciutto, thinly sliced and cut into ribbons

½ cup Parmesan, freshly grated

½ cup panko bread crumbs

¼ cup chives, chopped

1. Preheat oven to 350°F.

2. Butter a baking dish and set aside. Microwave potatoes on high for 8–10 minutes. Remove and set aside until cool enough to handle.

3. Place a par-cooked potato horizontal on a cutting board. Using a serrated knife, make slits in each potato, leaving about ¼-inch spaces in between each cut and also leaving about a ½-inch of the potato uncut on the bottom. (Tip: rest two wooden spoons on both sides of the potato to guide your knife and to prevent it from cutting through the bottom.) Repeat with remaining potatoes.

4. Place the potatoes in the prepared baking dish. Cut the sliced Gruyère cheese to fit into the cuts made in the potatoes, and stuff all of the potatoes. Season the potatoes with salt and pepper. Whisk the sour cream, milk, and nutmeg together in a bowl and season with salt and pepper. Pour mixture over the stuffed potatoes. Combine the prosciutto, Parmesan, and bread crumbs in a bowl. Sprinkle over the top of the potatoes. Scatter butter over the top of the potatoes. Place in the oven and bake for 35–40 minutes, or until golden brown on top and the potatoes are cooked through and crispy. Remove and garnish with fresh-chopped chives.

Old-Fashioned Cocktail

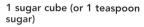

Serves: 1   Prep Time: 5 minutes

1 sugar cube (or 1 teaspoon sugar)

1 tablespoon water

2 dashes bitters

2½ ounces bourbon

1 strip orange peel

1 maraschino cherry

In the bottom of a chilled old-fashioned glass, add the sugar cube and a teaspoon of water. Using a wooden muddler, pulverize the sugar cube, breaking up the crystals to create a syrup. Add 2 dashes bitters. Fill the glass with ice, add the bourbon, and stir well. To garnish, twist the orange peel over the glass and top with a cherry.

C vs. C Casserole Champion

Blender Flan

Serves: 6   Prep Time: 1 hour   Cook Time: 35 minutes

Flan is one of the first desserts that a young chef learns how to make in cooking school. When plated, it's an impressive display of culinary talent, sure to sway even the most fickle of dinner guests. You'll have them believing that you were up all night putting together this tasty treasure, **it's just that good!** No one has to know how easily you whipped up this classic custard. Honey, your secret's safe with me.

FOR THE ROSEMARY ORANGE CARAMEL:

2 cups water

2 rosemary sprigs

½ orange, zested in large strips

1 cup granulated sugar

FOR THE CUSTARD:

8 ounces cream cheese, softened

½ cup granulated sugar

14 ounces sweetened condensed milk

1 cup evaporated milk

6 eggs, room temperature

1 tablespoon orange juice

2 teaspoons vanilla extract

½ teaspoon salt

1. Preheat oven to 350°F.

FOR THE ROSEMARY ORANGE CARAMEL:

2. Bring water to a boil in a small pot. Add the rosemary and orange zest, and reduce to a simmer. Cook until water has reduced by half. Pour mixture through a strainer, reserving water and discarding rosemary and zest.

3. Return water to the pot and add sugar, stir to dissolve over medium heat. Increase heat to medium-high and cook until mixture turns golden brown, about 10 minutes. Remove from heat and evenly distribute between 12 ramekins, swirling each to evenly coat the bottom. Set in a baking dish or roasting pan to rest.

FOR THE CUSTARD:

4. Combine the ingredients in a blender and process on low until evenly smooth. Do not overmix. Divide the mixture between the 12 ramekins with caramel. Fill the baking dish or roasting pan with enough water to come halfway up the ramekins.

5. Bake for 25–30 minutes, until custard is slightly jiggly and a toothpick comes out clean when inserted into the center. Remove from the oven and allow to cool in the water for 10 minutes.

6. Remove from water and dry ramekins before placing in the fridge to cool for at least 1 hour.

7. To serve, loosen flan with a paring knife that you run around the edges of the ramekin. Flip each onto a plate, topping with any caramel left in the ramekin.

Citrus Crostata

Serves: 8-10   **Prep Time: 30 minutes**   **Cook Time: 2½ hours-3 hours**

I have to say that pastry isn't my forte. All chefs have a weakness, and if I were forced to admit one, mine would be baking. So, if you find this free-form Italian pie too daunting, I give you my full blessing to run to the store, grab a jar of marmalade (or any other kind of jam) and a box of piecrust, and have at it. Either way this dish is **best eaten just as my _nonna_ did:** in the garden, in the late afternoon, with a glass of vin santo.

FOR THE CROSTATA DOUGH:

2½ cups cake flour, plus more for dusting

3 tablespoons sugar

½ teaspoon salt

Zest of 1 lemon

1 cup cold unsalted butter, cut into small cubes

¼ cup ice water, plus more if needed

FOR THE MARMALADE:

2 large pink grapefruit

5 Meyer lemons

4 cups sugar

2 cups water

1 teaspoon salt

Sour cream to garnish

1. Preheat the oven to 365°F.

FOR THE CROSTATA DOUGH:

2. Combine the flour, sugar, salt, and lemon zest in a food processor. Add the butter and zap quickly until the mixture resembles coarse crumbs. Add the ice water, 1 tablespoon at a time, and zap until the dough just forms a ball without being too wet or sticky.

3. Remove the dough from the processor and pat it into a flat disk, about 2 inches thick. Wrap it in plastic wrap and refrigerate for at least 30 minutes.

FOR THE MARMALADE:

4. Cut the fruits in half lengthwise and remove the seeds. Cut each grapefruit into 4 pieces. Place the seeds in a cheesecloth and tie up.

5. Slice the fruits into thin slices (skin included). Combine the fruit, sugar, water, and salt in a heavy-bottomed pot with the cheesecloth. Bring to a boil and then reduce to simmer.

6. Cook for 1½–2 hours at a very gentle simmer, skimming off foam occasionally, until the fruit is soft and translucent and the consistency of a loose jam.

7. Remove from heat. Discard the cheesecloth and seeds. Let it cool completely.

8. When ready to form the crostata, remove the dough from the refrigerator and allow it to soften enough to roll out. Sprinkle your work surface and a rolling pin lightly with cake flour.

9. Roll the dough out into a large circle, about ¼-inch thick. If the dough tears, press the edges back together.

10. Spoon the marmalade into the dough. Fold in the edges of the dough, leaving a 6-inch area of fruit exposed in the center.

11. Brush the tart with the liquid from the marmalade. Bake for 45 minutes, or until the crostata is golden brown. Serve the crostata warm or at room temperature, with a dollop of sour cream on each serving.

Fig Upside Down Cake

Serves: 8–10   Prep Time: 10 minutes   Cook Time: 40 minutes

Okay, people! Let's talk about upside down cake for a minute: warm caramel-soaked fruit atop rich, moist cake . . . my mouth is watering just thinking about it. This cake is such a crowd-pleaser, and if you follow my simple formula for success, you'll be eating this dish year-round. All right, guys, let's do the math!

Caramel + Fruit + Cake Batter = Pure Perfection.

So . . . if it's winter, use oranges; in the spring, try rhubarb. In summer—I say it's peaches. And in the fall, that's right, go on and get *figgy* with it!

2 sticks plus 3 tablespoons unsalted butter, at room temperature

⅔ cup light brown sugar, packed

1 lemon

1 orange, zest and juice

1 pound fresh figs, ends trimmed, cut in half

1½ cups all-purpose flour

1½ teaspoons baking powder

½ teaspoon salt

1 cup granulated sugar

4 large eggs at room temperature

⅓ cup sour cream

1 teaspoon vanilla extract

Whipped cream and powdered sugar, for garnish

1. Preheat oven to 350°F. Grease a 9-inch round cake pan.

2. In a small saucepan over medium heat, melt 3 tablespoons of butter. Add the brown sugar, juice of half a lemon, and juice of half an orange, and stir until everything is dissolved, about 2–3 minutes.

3. Scrape this mixture into the bottom of the prepared pan. Arrange the cut figs flesh-side down in an even layer on top of the brown sugar mixture in a circular pattern.

4. In a large bowl, whisk together the orange zest, flour, baking powder, and salt. In a separate bowl, cream together the 2 sticks of butter with the granulated sugar. Beat in the eggs, one at a time, then beat in the sour cream and vanilla. Then stir the dry mixture into the wet mixture with a wooden spoon.

5. Using a large spoon, carefully dollop the batter over the figs in the cake pan. Transfer to the oven and bake until the cake is golden brown and a toothpick inserted into the center comes out clean, about 40 minutes. Let rest in the cake pan for about 10 minutes. Then run a knife around the edges and invert the cake onto a platter. Cool completely before serving.

6. Serve with a dollop of whipped cream and a sprinkle of powdered sugar.

The Chew: An Essential Guide to Cooking and Entertaining

Cake Batter Bark

Serves: 15   Prep Time: 40 minutes   Cook Time: 10 minutes

Listen, when I'm throwing a party, I always make a party favor to give to my guests as a thank-you for coming. I think it's a really important part of entertaining. Now, I understand that after setting the table, and getting the cocktails ready, and cooking for a crowd, the last thing you want to think about is a parting gift. I get it. That's why **this cake batter bark is so perfect.** It's super easy and *soooooo* good. I like to fill little cellophane bags with the bark, tie them with some colorful string, and set them by the door for my guests to grab on their way out.

1 pound dark chocolate, roughly chopped

¾ pound white chocolate, roughly chopped

¼ cup yellow cake mix

¼ cup rainbow sprinkles

1. Line a baking sheet with parchment paper.

2. Place the dark chocolate in a bowl over a double boiler and melt. You can melt in the microwave, as well; just stir every minute or so. Pour the melted chocolate onto the baking sheet, spreading to create an even layer.

3. Meanwhile, melt the white chocolate in a bowl over a double boiler. Add in the cake mix and stir until fully combined.

4. Drizzle over the dark chocolate. Using a spatula, swirl the white chocolate throughout the dark. Top with the sprinkles. Place in the freezer for 30 minutes. Remove and break into pieces. Refrigerate in an airtight container until ready to eat.

Chocolate Phyllo Tart

Serves: 6   Prep Time: 2 hours   Cook Time: 30 minutes

If you haven't worked up to making your own piecrust from scratch, don't worry about it . . . you'll get there. Until then, **phyllo is a great alternative.** It's flaky and crunchy and holds up so nicely here to the chocolate. And when I say chocolate, I mean *chocolate!* This tart has chocolate ganache, chocolate pudding, and is topped with huge curls of chocolate. So, if you love chocolate—this is the dessert for you.

½ cup sugar

1 tablespoon cinnamon

4 sheets phyllo dough

½ cup butter, melted, plus more for preparing the pan

½ cup heavy cream

1 cup semisweet chocolate chips

Whipped cream, to garnish

3–4 ounces bittersweet chocolate, shaved, for garnish

FOR THE CHOCOLATE CREAM FILLING:

3 tablespoons cornstach

1 tablespoon flour

3 egg yolks, at room temperature

⅓ cup granulated sugar

Pinch of salt

1¼ cups whole milk

1 tablespoon unsweetened cocoa powder

⅓ cup semisweet chocolate chips

1 teaspoon vanilla extract

1. Preheat the oven to 350°F.

2. In a small bowl, mix together the sugar and cinnamon and set aside.

3. Prepare a rectangular tart pan with a removable bottom by buttering all the edges.

4. Working quickly and covering any unused phyllo dough with a slightly damp towel, begin to build the tart. Start by taking a sheet of the dough and laying it flat in front of you with the longest edge closest to you. Brush it fully with butter, and sprinkle some of the cinnamon and sugar mixture on top. Fold the dough into thirds by taking the edge closest to you and folding upward. Brush with more butter. Lay the sheet in the tart pan so that it is the length of the pan and covers a little more than half of the width. The dough should also come up a little over the sides.

5. Repeat the butter, sugaring, and folding process with another sheet of the dough. This time lay the folded sheet so that it covers the opposite side of the tart pan and overlaps the first layer. Continue this process with the remaining two sheets, alternating layering them from side to side of the pan so that an even layer is created.

6. Place the tart pan on a baking sheet and bake in the oven for 20 minutes, or until golden brown. Remove from oven and let cool.

7. Meanwhile, add ½ cup of heavy cream in a small saucepot. When the cream just starts to simmer, remove from heat and add the chocolate chips. Let stand for a minute and then stir together to combine until the chocolate is melted and fully incorporated.

8. Pour into the bottom of the cooled phyllo and spread evenly with an offset spatula. Pour the cooled chocolate filling (see step 11) on top and gently spread with an offset spatula.

9. Refrigerate for at least 2 hours.

FOR THE CHOCOLATE CREAM FILLING:

10. In a large saucepan off the heat, whisk together cornstarch, flour, egg yolks, sugar, and salt. Add in the milk and whisk until combined. Place the pot over medium heat and stir continuously until the mixture has thickened, about 7–10 minutes. Remove from heat and immediately add in cocoa powder, chocolate chips, and vanilla, stirring to combine. Remove from saucepan into a bowl and lay a piece of plastic wrap directly on the filling. Allow to cool before using.

11. To serve, remove the pie from the tart pan; then cut into 6 equal pieces. Top with whipped cream, and using a vegetable peeler, shave chocolate pieces from the block of chocolate directly onto the bars.

ARRANGING THE PERFECT BUFFET TABLE

Throwing a dinner party can be very stressful especially around the holidays. I find that if you're feeding more than eight people, a buffet is the way to go. I have created the perfect guide for mapping out your buffet table so that you can easily feed a crowd without breaking a sweat. —CLINTON KELLY

1. Stack plates at the start of the buffet.

2. If possible, set up the buffet with two sides to alleviate conjestion.

3. The buffet should move from hot to cold, starting with the main attraction.

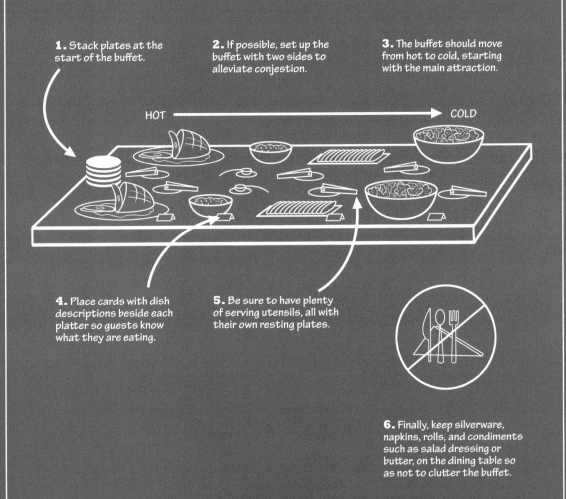

HOT ⟶ COLD

4. Place cards with dish descriptions beside each platter so guests know what they are eating.

5. Be sure to have plenty of serving utensils, all with their own resting plates.

6. Finally, keep silverware, napkins, rolls, and condiments such as salad dressing or butter, on the dining table so as not to clutter the buffet.

VIEWER Q&A
with CLINTON KELLY

• •

If you weren't doing what you are doing now (as a career), what would you be doing? —Teresa Acosta, Canton, OH

I am a trained journalist and I love writing. In fact, before I got into television I was a magazine editor. It turns out that my dream job is not much different than what I do now.

How much would they have to pay you to wear orange Crocs? —Krystina Mae, Emmaus, PA

Ha, this one cracks me up! Seriously, you'd have to pay me at least $10 million a year. I'd basically do anything for that much money. I love Mario, but he can keep his Crocs!

What do you always have in your fridge? —Patty Allende, Boynton Beach, FL

I always have milk, yogurt, tonic water, white wine, and cheese on hand. My fridge has everything one needs for an impromptu cocktail party.

COMFORT

No matter what culture you come from, comfort food really conjures up strong emotions and memories for everyone. It's about being around the table with the people you love—or being transported to a place where someone who loves you cooks for you. It can be that soothing stew that sits on the stove all day long in your mama's kitchen or the cheesy casserole that you bring out when the kids come home from soccer practice. Child, if it takes you to a special place, well that's comfort! For me, the perfect comfort meal means I'm out in the backyard with good friends and family, nothing to do but sit around and eat . . . fried chicken, salad, grilled veggies, eggs, grits, waffles, and lemonade. There is jazz playing in the background, maybe some R & B, and I'm in heaven!

—CARLA HALL

CLASSICS

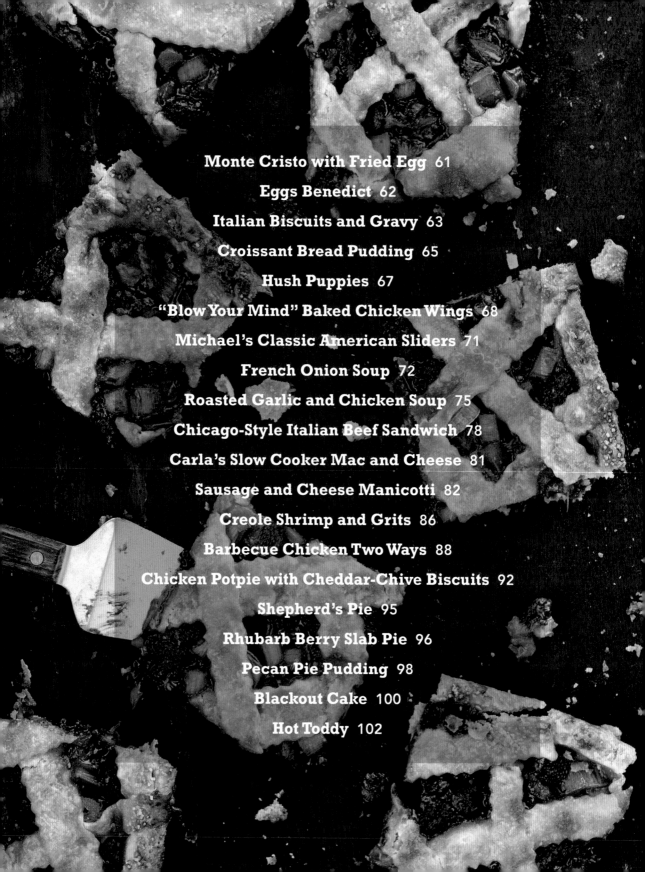

Monte Cristo with Fried Egg

Serves: 4   **Prep Time:** *10 minutes*   **Cook Time:** *5 minutes*

This sandwich is sheer madness when you think about it. A turkey, ham, and cheese sandwich that is battered and deep-fried, and then served with jam and a fried egg on top? You're probably saying, "What is he thinking?" Well, I'm thinking that it is unbelievably delicious and so comforting on a Sunday morning for brunch. **My kids love it!**

FOR THE MONTE CRISTO:

Vegetable oil, for frying

1 egg, lightly beaten

¾ cup milk

¾ cup flour

2 teaspoons baking powder

Salt and freshly ground black pepper, to taste

8 slices thick-cut white bread

2 tablespoons mustard

4 slices deli ham

4 slices smoked turkey

4 Fontina cheese slices

16 pickled jalapeños, optional

Powdered sugar for garnish

4 tablespoons strawberry jam, divided (1 per sandwich)

FOR THE FRIED EGGS:

4 eggs

1 tablespoon butter

1. In a large cast-iron skillet, preheat 2 inches vegetable oil to 365°F.

2. In a shallow baking dish, whisk together the egg and milk. Stir in the flour and baking powder, then season with salt and pepper.

3. Spread mustard on the bread slices and make a sandwich with the ham, turkey, and Fontina. (Add pickled jalapeños, if desired.)

4. Coat the sandwiches evenly on all sides with the batter. Drop into the oil, and fry until golden brown and crisp, about 2 minutes per side.

5. Remove to a paper towel–lined plate, sprinkle with powdered sugar, and serve with a spoonful of your favorite jam.

6. While the sandwiches cool slightly, heat the butter in a nonstick skillet over medium heat. Once the butter has foamed and subsided, crack each egg into the skillet and fry until the yolk is set, about 3 or 4 minutes.

7. Serve a fried egg alongside each Monte Cristo.

Eggs Benedict

Serves: 4   Prep Time: 10 minutes   Cook Time: 25 minutes

You know the feeling: you've been good all week long, and by the weekend you just can't eat another salad or grilled chicken breast. That's when I turn to my favorite over-the-top brunch classic . . . eggs Benedict. Usually I make this on Sunday when I'm just a teeny, tiny bit hungover; and **it always makes me feel better**, especially paired with a mimosa or Bloody Mary. With or without a little hair of the dog, this dish is so satisfying.

3 tablespoons distilled vinegar

8 large eggs

1 tablespoon unsalted butter

8 slices Canadian bacon

4 plain English muffins, split

1 tablespoon chives, finely chopped, for garnish

FOR THE HOLLANDAISE SAUCE:

4 tablespoons lemon juice

8 egg yolks

¼ teaspoon salt

Dash of hot sauce

1 cup butter, melted

White pepper

1. Pour enough water into a low-sided saucepot to reach about 3 inches up the sides, and add the vinegar. Bring to a gentle simmer over medium heat. Crack an egg into a cup and carefully slide it into the hot poaching liquid. Quickly repeat with all the eggs. Poach the eggs, stirring them occasionally with a spoon, until the whites are firm but the yolks are soft, or to the desired degree of doneness, about 3–5 minutes. Using a slotted spoon, remove the eggs and transfer to a kitchen towel. Lightly dab the eggs with the towel to remove any excess water.

2. While the eggs are poaching, melt the butter in a large skillet over medium heat. Add the Canadian bacon and cook until heated through, about a minute on each side.

3. In a blender, add the lemon juice, egg yolks, salt, and a dash of hot sauce. Remove the center section of the blender lid, and with the blender on its lowest setting, blend for 20 seconds. Add the butter, pouring it into the blender in a very thin stream. Once incorporated, season with white pepper.

4. To serve, toast the English muffin halves and divide them among 4 warmed plates. Top each half with a slice of Canadian bacon, and set an egg on top. Spoon the hollandaise sauce over the eggs and garnish with the chives. Serve immediately.

Italian Biscuits and Gravy

Serves: 12   **Prep Time:** 15 minutes   **Cook Time:** 40 minutes

When I think of Southern food, I can't help thinking of biscuits and gravy. Of course, I have to put my Italian spin on everything I touch, and this southern staple is no exception. For the "biscuits," I use an Italian flatbread called *piadina*, from the Emilia-Romagna region of Italy. This dough is slightly easier to make than a biscuit because it comes together so quickly, right in your food processor. For the gravy, of course, we use Italian sausage (what else?) and prosciutto. **This dish is the perfect marriage** of Italian ingredients and American technique.

FOR THE PIADINA DOUGH:

4½ cups cake flour, plus more for dusting

1 tablespoon baking soda

1 teaspoon salt

⅔ cup lard or butter, cut into cubes

¾–1 cup ice water

FOR THE SAUSAGE GRAVY:

1 pound spicy Italian sausage, out of the casing

1½ cups milk

2 tablespoons flour

4 slices prosciutto, cut into thin ribbons

1 teaspoon salt

Pinch of freshly grated nutmeg

1. Combine the flour, baking soda, and salt in a food processor and pulse to combine. Scatter the pieces of lard or butter over the flour and pulse just until incorporated. With the motor running, add the water and process just until the dough begins to clump together.

2. Turn the dough out onto a floured surface and roll to ¼-inch to ½-inch thick.

3. Heat griddle to medium heat.

4. Cut the dough into 3-inch rounds.

5. Working in batches, place the rounds on the griddle and cook until light golden brown on the first side, about 1–2 minutes. Turn and repeat on the other side.

FOR THE SAUSAGE GRAVY:

6. In a sauté pan over medium heat, slowly cook the sausage, allowing it to render all of its fat. Cook, crumbling with a wooden spoon, until sausage is crisp and dark brown, about 10–15 minutes.

7. Warm milk in a small saucepot or in the microwave.

8. Add the flour and, using a wooden spoon, stir vigorously. Slowly add the milk, stirring continuously to prevent clumping, and stir in the prosciutto. Bring sauce to a boil and cook until sauce has thickened and reduced slightly, then remove from heat. Season with salt and nutmeg. Serve the sausage gravy over the *piadina*.

Croissant Bread Pudding

Serves: 8   **Prep Time:** 40 minutes   **Cook Time:** 1 hour

When you're a busy parent, there are never enough hours in the day. And with everything your kids have scheduled—and everything on your to-do list—the last thing you have time for is entertaining. Well, not anymore. I find that the trick to "juggling" it all is simply upgrading store-bought items, a simple step that allows you to **spend less time in the kitchen**, while still yielding stellar results. In this brunch classic, I use store-bought croissants and chocolate-hazelnut spread, and believe me when I tell you this comforting combination brings out the kid in everyone.

2 tablespoons butter

6 croissants, cut into thirds

2 bananas, sliced, plus more to garnish

3 eggs

1½ cups heavy cream

1 cup milk

1 teaspoon vanilla

Pinch of salt

1 cup chocolate-hazelnut spread, divided

1. Preheat oven to 350°F. Butter a 9x9 baking dish.

2. Place the cut croissants into the baking dish so they fit snug. Sprinkle in the cut pieces of banana and push to fall between the pieces of croissant.

3. Whisk together the eggs, cream, milk, vanilla, and salt. Add half of the chocolate-hazelnut spread and whisk to combine. Pour over the croissants. Let stand at room temperature for 30 minutes. Cover with aluminum foil and place in the oven to bake until the custard is set, about 45 minutes. Uncover and cook for an additional 15 minutes.

4. Remove and let rest for 15 minutes before serving. Garnish with a few pieces of bananas and a warm drizzle of the remaining chocolate-hazelnut spread.

CLINTON'S "WHO KNEW?" TIP
Hey guys, don't throw away those banana peels! Did you know that you can polish your shoes with them? That's right, it's not a substitute for a good shoeshine, but if you find yourself in desperate need of a polish, just rub your shoe with the inside of that peel and then buff with a towel. You'll be good to go in no time!

Hush Puppies

Serves: 6–8 **Prep Time:** 10 minutes **Cook Time:** 5 minutes

When I was growing up in the South, hush puppies were everywhere. You ate them with fried fish, fried chicken, or just as an appetizer with an herby sauce. They are basically just little spoonfuls of corn bread, but gussied up with some spices and seasonings that make them little pillows of goodness. More than any other food, **these really take me back to my childhood.**

FOR THE HUSH PUPPIES:

2 cups yellow cornmeal

1 cup all-purpose flour

1 teaspoon baking powder

½ teaspoon baking soda

¾ teaspoon kosher salt

¼ teaspoon paprika

¼ teaspoon black pepper

Pinch of cayenne pepper

1 large onion, finely diced

2 eggs, slightly beaten

1–1¼ cups buttermilk

2 cloves garlic, minced

2 tablespoons bacon fat, melted

Vegetable oil for frying

FOR THE DIPPING SAUCE:

½ cup mayonnaise

¼ cup sour cream

1 lemon, zest and juice

1 teaspoon seafood seasoning

1 teaspoon parsley, chopped

1 teaspoon dill, chopped

½ teaspoon thyme, chopped

½ teaspoon paprika

Salt and freshly ground black pepper, to taste

FOR THE HUSH PUPPIES:

1. Combine dry ingredients, then add diced onion. In a separate bowl, combine eggs, buttermilk, garlic, and melted bacon fat. Stir wet ingredients into dry just until combined. Do not overmix. Fry rounded teaspoonfuls in oil preheated to 350°F for 3–4 minutes, until golden brown.

FOR THE DIPPING SAUCE:

2. In a medium bowl, stir together the ingredients and adjust seasoning to taste. Serve with the hush puppies.

"Blow Your Mind" Baked Chicken Wings

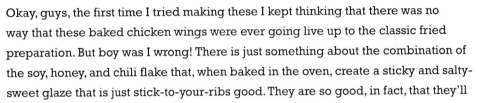

Serves: 8   Prep Time: 2 hours   Cook Time: 30 minutes

Okay, guys, the first time I tried making these I kept thinking that there was no way that these baked chicken wings were ever going live up to the classic fried preparation. But boy was I wrong! There is just something about the combination of the soy, honey, and chili flake that, when baked in the oven, create a sticky and salty-sweet glaze that is just stick-to-your-ribs good. They are so good, in fact, that they'll **blow your mind!**

2 teaspoons cornstarch

2 tablespoons coconut oil

3 garlic cloves, minced

1 tablespoon grated fresh ginger

3 scallions, sliced; whites and greens separated

¼ cup low-sodium soy sauce

½ cup honey

2 limes, juiced

1 tablespoon sesame oil

2 teaspoons chili flakes

2 pounds chicken wings, separated; tips removed

Salt and freshly ground black pepper, to taste

1. Preheat oven to 350°F.

2. Season chicken wings with salt and pepper, and place in a rimmed baking dish. Bake for 20 minutes and set aside.

3. In a small bowl, make a slurry with the cornstarch and a tablespoon of water, and set aside.

4. Heat 2 tablespoons of coconut oil in a sauté pan over medium-low heat. Toss in the garlic, ginger, and scallion whites, cooking for 30 seconds or until fragrant.

5. Stir in the soy sauce, honey, lime juice, sesame oil, and chili flakes. Whisk in the cornstarch slurry and bring to a boil. Reduce to a simmer and cook for 3–4 minutes until sauce has thickened slightly. Remove from heat and allow to cool to room temperature.

6. Pour sauce over wings and return to the oven for 20 minutes or until wings are cooked through and sauce is sticky.

7. Remove from oven and allow to cool slightly before serving. Garnish with reserved scallion greens.

Michael's Classic American Sliders

Serves: 8   **Prep Time:** 15 minutes   **Cook Time:** 12–15 minutes

Do you know why we Americans call these delicious mini-burgers "sliders"? Well, when you build the burger on the griddle, you stack it. First the burger patty, then the onions, then you lay the bottom bun on top of the burger, and the top bun on top of the bottom bun, and then you slide it up to the top of the griddle where it sits and steams the bun. If you want to **impress your friends**, next time you're at one of those old-school burger joints, just ask for a "lid" on your burger . . . that means with cheese!

Extra-virgin olive oil

1 white onion, thinly sliced

Salt and freshly ground black pepper, to taste

1 pound ground beef, separated into 2-ounce balls

5 slices American cheese, cut in half, then folded in half to make a square

8 potato dinner rolls

Bread-and-butter pickle slices for garnish

1. Preheat a griddle over medium-high heat. When hot, add a drizzle of olive oil and the sliced onions. Season with salt and pepper, and cook, stirring occasionally until tender and translucent, about 5 or 6 minutes. Push the onions to one side of the griddle and let cook until slightly caramelized. Place rounded patties down, leaving space in between each one.

2. Using the back of a spatula, smash balls into even, thin patties and season with salt and pepper. Add a small pile of the griddled onions on top of each patty, pressing down gently. Cook for 2–3 minutes until a nice golden crust forms. Flip the patties over, onion-side down.

3. Continue to cook for another 2 minutes. Meanwhile, add the cheese on top of the patties, then place the bottom bun facedown on top of the cheese; next place the top bun on top of the bottom bun. (The buns will soften and steam while the sliders cook.)

4. Remove the sliders to a platter and place top bun on top of the onion-griddled side. Serve sliders alongside sliced pickles.

CARLA'S "SLIDER" TIP

Hey guys, did you know that you can make sliders for a crowd using a muffin tin? That's right, just preheat your oven to 450°F, and heat up two muffin tins. Press your slider patties into each muffin mold, top with the other hot muffin tin and bake for about 6–8 minutes. You've got 12 patties ready to go without breaking a sweat!

French Onion Soup

Serves: 6   **Prep Time:** 15 minutes   **Cook Time:** 1 hour, 30 minutes

Last season, we did an entire show dedicated to our viewers. In that show, we asked you what hearty, feel-good dishes you wanted *The Chew* Crew to make: and this French classic was top of the list! **It's like a little Parisian vacation** right in your own home, and definitely something I make when the weather starts to cool off. I like to pour the soup into individual ramekins before any guests arrive; and then right before it's time for dinner, I top with a crouton—overflowing with Gruyère cheese—and pop right in the oven until it's bubbly and oozing cheesy goodness.

2 pounds medium yellow onions, sliced

½ bunch fresh thyme, tied with kitchen twine

2 bay leaves

1 teaspoon salt

2 tablespoons unsalted butter

2 tablespoons olive oil

1 tablespoon all-purpose flour

1 cup full-bodied red wine

4 cups reduced-sodium chicken broth

1 cup water

1 teaspoon black pepper

6 slices baguette, ½-inch slices

½ pound Gruyère or mild Swiss cheese, grated

2 tablespoons Parmesan, grated

1. Preheat broiler to high.

2. In a heavy pot or Dutch oven, cook onions, thyme, bay leaves, salt, butter, and olive oil over moderate heat for about 45 minutes, stirring frequently, until onions are a deep caramel color.

3. Add flour and stir; cook for about 1 more minute. Stir in wine and cook for about 2 minutes.

4. Stir in broth, water, and black pepper and bring to a boil. Then reduce to a simmer and cook, uncovered, another 30 minutes, stirring occasionally.

5. When ready to serve, toast baguette slices.

6. Remove bay leaves and thyme stems from soup. Ladle soup into oven-safe crocks or bowls. Top with toasted baguette slice, then grated Gruyère and Parmesan.

7. Broil until cheese bubbles and turns light golden brown, about 1 minute.

Roasted Garlic and Chicken Soup

Serves: 6   Prep Time: 30 minutes   Cook Time: 20 minutes

This is the perfect recipe to **keep you happy, healthy, and strong** all winter long. I love to keep a pot of this on the stove during the holidays when the entire family is packed under one roof, to make sure we all stay healthy enough to open presents Christmas morning! I basically take a classic chicken soup and amp it up with a little bit of jalapeño, roasted garlic, and ginger, which are all great immune-boosting ingredients.

1½ cups farro, rinsed

2 heads garlic

Olive oil

Salt, to taste

6 cups chicken broth

1 yellow onion, diced

2 medium carrots, peeled and sliced into coins

1 jalapeño, thinly sliced

1 inch fresh ginger, peeled and minced

2 cups leftover shredded chicken

1 lemon, juiced

1. Preheat oven to 400°F.

2. Cook farro according to package instructions and set aside. This can be done a few days in advance and stored in an airtight container in the fridge.

3. Cut garlic bulbs crosswise to remove the tops and expose cloves. Place the cut bulbs on a large piece of aluminum foil and drizzle with olive oil and salt. Gather the edges of the aluminum and press together to completely encapsulate the garlic. Bake for 30 minutes.

4. Remove garlic from oven and carefully open up the package. Garlic cloves should be soft and golden. Squeeze out the softened cloves from the bulb, discarding skins. Blend garlic into the chicken broth using an immersion blender or traditional blender. Set aside.

5. Heat a large Dutch oven over medium heat with a few tablespoons of olive oil. Sauté the onion and carrots, seasoning with salt, until soft and translucent, about 7 minutes. Add sliced jalapeños and cook for 2 minutes or until soft. Stir in ginger and cook just until fragrant.

6. Stir in the garlicky chicken broth and parsley. Add cooked farro, shredded chicken, and lemon juice. Adjust seasoning to taste.

7. Serve warm.

The CHEW

Chicago-Style Italian Beef Sandwich

Serves: 12   Prep Time: 2 hours   Cook Time: 1 hour, 20 minutes

When I head out to Chicago, **one of my must-eat treats** is this classic Italian hero. This sandwich is big enough to satisfy any appetite, but the true genius behind this masterpiece is the giardiniera. This heavenly, spicy concoction of celery and peppers gives the sandwich some acidity that really balances out the fattiness of the beef. If you can't get away to the Windy City, my version is just as good.

4 pounds boneless prime rib roast

Freshly cracked black pepper

12 soft Italian-style hoagie rolls

FOR THE RUB:

1 tablespoon kosher salt

1½ teaspoons onion powder

1 tablespoon fresh oregano

1 teaspoon paprika

5 cloves garlic

2 tablespoons extra-virgin olive oil

FOR THE AU JUS DIPPING SAUCE:

2½ cups low-sodium beef stock

FOR THE SPICY CELERY GIARDINIERA:

1 pound celery, sliced thin on a bias

½ cup jalapeños, thinly sliced into rings

2 tablespoons Fresno chiles, thinly sliced into rings

2 cloves garlic, minced

1 cup red onion, thinly sliced

1 teaspoon ancho chili powder

2 teaspoons kosher salt

1 teaspoon freshly ground black pepper

1. Combine all of the rub ingredients in a small bowl or in a mortar and pestle. Use the end of a wooden spoon or a pestle to mash all of the ingredients together to make a fairly smooth paste. Season your roast with lots of cracked black pepper on all sides, then season with the rub mixture, covering the roast on all sides. Place the roast in the fridge to marinate for 4 hours or up to overnight.

2. Remove the roast from the fridge and let come to room temperature. Preheat your oven to 450°F.

3. Place the beef in a roasting rack inside of a roasting pan, fat-side up.

4. Place the prime rib in the oven for 30 minutes. Then, without opening, lower the oven temperature to 325°F and continue to roast until internal temperature reaches 120°F, about 50 minutes. Remove the roast from the oven and place it on a cutting board or platter, tented with foil.

5. Leave the thermometer in while letting the roast rest for 20–30 minutes, allowing the temperature to rise to 130°F, for a perfect medium rare.

6. Meanwhile, place the same roasting pan over a stove-top burner on low heat. Add the beef stock and scrape all of the bits off the bottom of the pan. Add any meat juices from the resting roast as well. Keep the liquid warm until ready to serve. Slice the roast into paper-thin slices. Set aside in the warm jus.

FOR THE SPICY CELERY GIARDINIERA:

7. Mix all the ingredients together. Refrigerate for 2–24 hours.

1 tablespoon dried oregano

1 tablespoon coriander seeds, toasted and ground

¼ cup flat-leaf parsley, chopped

4 ounces red wine vinegar

4 ounces extra-virgin olive oil

TO BUILD THE SANDWICHES:

8. Take a hoagie roll and split it in half lengthwise, not cutting all the way through. Quickly dip the cut side into the warm beef broth. Add a heaping pile of the sliced beef followed by some of the spicy celery giardiniera. Slice in half. Enjoy immediately!

Carla's Slow Cooker Mac and Cheese

Serves: 4   Prep Time: 10 minutes   Cook Time: 4–6 hours

Mac and cheese is one of those **classic comfort dishes** that most of us grew up with, and when I need a hug, I turn to this version because it tastes just like the one from my youth. I love this dish so much because I can literally toss everything together in the morning before I leave the house, pour it into my slow cooker, and when I walk in the door at the end of the day, I've got a delicious meal ready to put on the table.

½ pound macaroni noodles

1½ cups half-and-half

4 ounces cream cheese (half a stick), cut into small pieces

1 teaspoon paprika

1 tablespoon Dijon

1 teaspoon cayenne pepper

1 teaspoon salt

½ teaspoon black pepper

1 egg

2 cups cheddar cheese, grated

2 cups pepper jack cheese, grated

1. Cook noodles 3 minutes less time than package instructions.

2. In a mixing bowl, combine half-and-half, cream cheese, paprika, Dijon, cayenne, salt, pepper, and egg. Whisk to combine.

3. Put cooked pasta into the slow cooker. Add grated cheeses and mix together. Pour egg and cream mixture over the pasta (liquid should cover most of the pasta).

4. Cook on low for 4–6 hours.

Sausage and Cheese Manicotti

Serves: 12   **Prep Time: 5 minutes**   **Cook Time: 45 minutes**

Let's face it, the holidays can be a little bit stressful at times. So I've created this **incredibly satisfying dish** that will help make your winter days jolly and bright. We like to make a lot of this, assembly-line style, at the Batali house in that stretch of time between Thanksgiving and Christmas so that we are prepared for the revolving door of guests that inevitably stop by in December.

2 pounds hot Italian sausage, loose

Extra-virgin olive oil

3 cups basic tomato sauce (see page 85)

1 package dried manicotti pasta

32 ounces fresh ricotta cheese, drained

2 cups freshly grated Parmesan, divided, plus more to serve

½ cup fresh classic basil pesto (see page 85)

1 egg, whisked

Salt and freshly ground black pepper, to taste

1. Preheat oven to 400°F. Oil a 9x13 baking dish.

2. In a large skillet, brown the sausage with a few tablespoons of olive oil over medium heat. Cook for 15–20 minutes, breaking the sausage up into small pieces, until dark and crispy. Pour in the basic tomato sauce and stir to combine. Remove from heat and allow to cool until ready to use.

3. Bring a large pot of salted water to a boil and cook the manicotti noodles 3 minutes short of the package's instructions. Drain and pat dry with a clean kitchen towel.

4. In a large bowl, stir together the ricotta, 1½ cups grated Parmesan, and pesto until fully combined. Stir in the egg and season with salt and pepper to taste. Transfer the filling to a piping bag or large zip-top bag. Cut the tip off the bag and pipe into the cooked pasta, filling each tube with the cheese mixture.

5. Place a single layer of the filled pasta in the prepared baking dish and top with some of the sauce. Repeat with another layer of filled pasta tubes and top with the remaining sauce. Sprinkle the remaining Parmesan over the dish and bake for 20–25 minutes, or until golden and dark in some spots on top. Remove from the oven and allow to cool for 10 minutes before serving. Garnish with more grated cheese if desired.

Basic Tomato Sauce

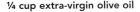

Makes: 1 quart   **Prep Time: 5 minutes**   **Cook Time: 45 minutes**

¼ cup extra-virgin olive oil

1 Spanish onion, ¼-inch dice

4 cloves garlic, thinly sliced

Salt and freshly ground black pepper, to taste

3 tablespoons chopped fresh thyme leaves (or 1 tablespoon dried thyme)

½ medium carrot, finely grated

2 cans peeled whole tomatoes (28 ounces each), crushed by hand, juices reserved

1. Add olive oil to a medium saucepan and place over medium heat.

2. Once hot, add the onion and garlic, and season with salt and pepper.

3. Sauté until translucent and slightly caramelized, about 8 to 10 minutes.

4. Add the thyme and carrot, and sauté for 5 more minutes.

5. Add the tomatoes and bring to a boil, stirring often. Lower the heat to a simmer. Cook for 30 minutes. Season with salt and pepper to taste.

Tip: Refrigerate the sauce in an airtight container for 1 week or freeze for up to 6 months.

Classic Basil Pesto

Serves: 6   **Prep Time: 10 minutes**

2½ cups basil leaves, chopped

2 cloves garlic

2 tablespoons pine nuts, raw

¼ cup Parmesan, freshly grated

¼ cup extra-virgin olive oil

Salt and freshly ground black pepper, to taste

1. In the bowl of a food processor, combine the garlic, basil, and pine nuts.

2. Pulse and chop until almost blended. Pulse a few times to chop and combine.

3. With the food processor running, drizzle in the olive oil until combined, The resulting pesto should be a little chunky and not too wet.

4. Add the grated Parmesan and pulse a couple times just to combine.

5. Season to taste with salt and pepper. Refrigerate up to 1 week.

Creole Shrimp and Grits

Serves: 4 **Prep Time:** *2 minutes* **Cook Time:** *10 minutes*

I am not southern; I'm from Long Island, New York. But I created this dish because I wanted to eat like a southerner (but didn't want to spend all day in the kitchen like a Southern grandma). So if you are a purist when it comes to southern cuisine, well, **you can kiss my grits** . . . kidding! This dish really is tasty. The shrimp gets a little bit crispy when you coat it in all those creole seasonings and then sauté it in that bacon fat—and then pour it over those cheesy grits. One bite and even the strictest of southerners will be clamoring for seconds.

¼ pound smoked bacon, chopped

1½ pounds extra-large domestic shrimp, peeled and deveined

2 tablespoons creole seasoning

2 garlic cloves, thinly sliced

¼ cup chicken stock

½ cup tomato puree

1 tablespoon chopped chives, for garnish

Hot sauce, to garnish

FOR THE GRITS:

2 cups instant yellow grits

½ cup freshly grated aged white cheddar cheese

¼ cup freshly grated Parmesan

1. In a large sauté pan, cook bacon over low heat. Cook until crispy, then remove bacon with a slotted spoon to a plate or platter.

2. With reserved bacon fat in the pan, increase heat to medium-high.

3. Sprinkle the creole seasoning on both sides of the shrimp. Add to the hot pan and cook for 1–2 minutes per side until opaque but not tough. Remove shrimp to the plate with the bacon.

4. Add the garlic and deglaze pan with stock. Reduce heat to medium-low and stir in the tomato puree. Cook for 5 minutes, or until thickened. Adjust seasoning to taste.

5. Return shrimp to the pan with sauce and toss to coat. Plate shrimp and sauce over grits. Garnish with chopped chives, bacon, and hot sauce.

FOR THE GRITS:

6. Cook grits according to package instructions. Stir in cheeses and adjust seasoning to taste.

Barbecue Chicken Two Ways

Serves: 8 **Prep Time: 45–50 minutes** **Cook Time: 30 minutes**

There really is no better way to celebrate summer with your family than with a good old-fashioned cookout. **I love barbecue chicken**; it's one of my go-to comfort dishes when it starts to get hot outside. Heck, I'd even make these dishes in the dead of winter! They are that good. With two totally different, yet simple marinades that both have unbelievably complex flavors, you'd better make extra . . . these babies go quick!

2 whole chickens, split in half down the backbone

Salt and freshly ground black pepper, to taste

¼ cup extra-virgin olive oil

2 tablespoons whole coriander, toasted and cracked

FOR THE ALABAMA WHITE BARBECUE SAUCE:

2 cups mayo

3 tablespoons freshly grated horseradish

4 tablespoons apple-cider vinegar

2 tablespoons fresh lemon juice

1 teaspoon granulated sugar

½ teaspoon cayenne

2 teaspoons kosher salt

4 teaspoons freshly ground black pepper

FOR THE THAI-STYLE BARBECUE SAUCE:

1½ cups unsweetened coconut milk

¼ cup minced red onion

1 tablespoon grated fresh ginger

¼ cup honey

2 lemons, halved

4 limes, halved

Olive oil

1. Season chicken with salt, pepper, and coriander.

2. Place two of the chicken halves in a baking dish and cover with half of the Alabama Sauce. Let marinate for 30 minutes. Reserve the other half of the sauce. Marinate the remaining chicken in Thai-Style Barbecue Sauce, reserving half for brushing.

3. Preheat grill to medium-high heat.

4. Drizzle the chickens with olive oil and place on the grill, skin-side down and close the lid. Cook for 10 minutes, flip all of the chicken over and cook for another 10 minutes. Then brush on a good amount of the Thai-Style Barbecue Sauce all over half of the marinated chicken. Brush the remaining chicken with a good amount of the Alabama White Barbecue Sauce. Close lid and cook for an additional 2 minutes. Remove the chicken to a cutting board, tent with foil, and let rest for 10 minutes.

5. Cut each chicken between the breast and the leg. Brush the 8 chicken pieces with more barbecue sauce and serve immediately.

FOR THE ALABAMA WHITE BARBECUE SAUCE:

Whisk or blend all the ingredients together until well combined. Refrigerate until ready to use. The flavors in the sauce will come out more as it sits.

FOR THE THAI-STYLE BARBECUE SAUCE:

Blend the coconut milk, red onion, ginger, and honey together until almost completely smooth. Then pour into a saucepot. Bring the mixture to a simmer and cook over medium-low heat for 30 minutes, until reduced and thickened. Pour into a mixing bowl and let cool.

1 tablespoon soy sauce

2 teaspoons fish sauce

¼ cup sambal

¼ cup cilantro, finely chopped, plus more for garnish

¼ cup scallion, finely chopped

Pinch of salt

Mint for garnish

¼ cup roasted peanuts, roughly chopped, for garnish

In the meantime, preheat grill to medium-high heat. Drizzle the lemon and limes with olive oil on the cut side. Place on the preheated grill, cut-side down, and grill for 5 minutes without moving until they are nicely charred with grill marks. Remove to a plate and set aside. Squeeze both citrus juices into the reduced sauce, followed by the soy sauce, fish sauce, sambal, herbs, and a pinch of salt. Refrigerate until ready to use. The flavors will come out more as the sauce sits.

MARIO'S "GRILL" TIP

You don't need all of those fancy grill tools to throw a great barbecue, especially when it comes to cleaning your grill. Just crinkle up a piece of tinfoil and wrap it around a pair of tongs. Rub the foil over the grill grates while the grill is still hot, and any leftover mess comes right off.

PAGES 90–91
Carla and Michael swap secrets with The Swedish Chef.

Chicken Potpie with Cheddar-Chive Biscuits

Serves: 8   Prep Time: 25 minutes   Cook Time: 30 minutes

Everyone knows how I feel about biscuits. If there is a biscuit in the room, I will find it and devour it. I just can't get enough of them. That's why I came up with this awesome chicken potpie that is really all about the biscuit. This cheddar and chive combo is just **so tangy and delicious**, and when you drop them on top of that potpie and bake them, the bottom turns into a pillowy dumpling, while the top gets golden and crunchy. One bite, and it's all about the happy dance.

FOR THE CHICKEN FILLING:

3 tablespoons extra-virgin olive oil

2 medium yellow onions, ½-inch dice

2 carrots, cut in half lengthwise, and then into ½-inch-thick half-moons

3 celery ribs, cut in half lengthwise, and then into ½-inch-thick slices on a bias

2 sprigs fresh thyme

2 sprigs fresh rosemary

2 fresh sage leaves

⅓ cup all-purpose flour

1 fresh or dried bay leaf

6 cups chicken stock

¾ cup heavy cream

1 store-bought rotisserie chicken, shredded

1 cup frozen baby peas

Salt and freshly ground black pepper, to taste

FOR THE CHEDDAR-CHIVE DROP BISCUITS:

2 cups all-purpose flour, plus more for dredging

2 teaspoons baking powder

2 teaspoons salt

6 tablespoons butter, cut into pats

---

1. Preheat oven to 400°F.

FOR THE CHICKEN FILLING:

2. In a deep cast-iron skillet, heat 3 tablespoons oil over medium-high heat. Sauté the onions, carrots, and celery with the thyme, rosemary, and sage for 15 minutes. Season with salt and pepper.

3. When the vegetables are fork-tender, remove herb stems and discard.

4. Whisk in the flour. Gradually pour in chicken stock while whisking. Add bay leaves and heavy cream. Bring the mixture to a boil and reduce to a simmer. Stir in peas and chicken. Simmer for 10 more minutes, or until thick and creamy. Adjust seasoning if necessary.

FOR THE CHEDDAR-CHIVE DROP BISCUITS:

5. Combine flour, baking powder, and salt in a large bowl.

6. Cut pats of butter into dry ingredients with fingertips until they resemble peas. Add the cheese and chives to the flour mixture and stir to combine.

7. In medium bowl, whisk together the yogurt and milk. Make a well in the dry ingredients and pour in the wet mixture. Using your hands or a wooden spoon, mix until just combined, adding more flour if necessary.

8. Drop large, heaping spoonfuls of dough, about ¼ cup each, onto a floured surface. Shake off the excess flour and then arrange the biscuits on top of the chicken potpie base. Bake for 30–35 minutes.

1¼ cups cheddar cheese

⅓ cup chives, chopped

½ cup yogurt

1⅓ cups milk

½ cup flour, for dredging

2 tablespoons of butter for finishing, optional

9. Once the biscuits are golden brown, remove the skillet from the oven. Place a pat of butter over each biscuit and allow to melt before serving.

Shepherd's Pie

Serves: 8   Prep Time: 30 minutes   Cook Time: 15 minutes

You don't have to wait for St. Patrick's Day to enjoy this Irish classic. This can be a delicious family meal **any night of the week**. For this dish, I took Irish bacon, which is uncured and a little less smoky—but still incredibly flavorful—and combined it with Irish sausage and veggies. Then I topped it with mashed potatoes. The outcome was decadent and delicious, and oh so Irish.

2 tablespoons olive oil

16 ounces Irish sausage or sweet Italian sausage, removed from casings

4 ounces bacon, chopped

2 carrots, peeled and cut in ½-inch-thick half-moons

2 leeks, split, chopped

1 ounce Irish whiskey (or regular whiskey)

3 tablespoons flour

1 cup chicken stock

1 cup peas, fresh or frozen

Salt and freshly ground black pepper, to taste

FOR THE MASHED POTATOES:

3 pounds Yukon gold potatoes, peeled

1 cup olive oil

1. Preheat broiler to medium-high.

2. In a cast-iron skillet, over medium heat, add the olive oil and sausage and cook until it has crisped and rendered its fat, about 10 minutes. Add the bacon and cook until crisp.

3. Add the carrots and leeks, cooking until the vegetables have softened. Deglaze the pan with whiskey.

4. Add the flour and cook until the flour has integrated and a wet sand texture forms. Add the peas and chicken stock. Bring to a boil, and then reduce to a simmer. Cook until the sauce comes together and thickens, about 10 minutes.

5. Pipe the mashed potatoes over the top of the filling and transfer to the oven. Broil for 10–15 minutes, or until golden brown and crisp.

FOR THE MASHED POTATOES:

1. Place potatoes in a large pot and cover with water by 3 inches. Bring to a boil and season with salt.

2. Cook for 15–20 minutes, or until fork-tender. Drain and set aside until cool enough to handle.

3. Press the potatoes through a ricer. Whisk in about 1 cup of olive oil. Transfer to a piping bag.

Rhubarb Berry Slab Pie

Serves: *16–20 people*   **Prep Time:** *40 minutes*   **Cook Time:** *30 minutes*

Are you one of those people that always wishes that there was just a little more crust to go with your pie? I've got you covered because this slab pie is **a crust lover's dream!** The crust gets really crispy on the bottom, but also soaks up some of the juices from the berries. And the top crust just adds that little bit of extra crunch that you're missing from other pies—and it feeds a ton of people. With this crowd-pleaser, you'll be the most popular parent at the bake sale.

FOR THE PIE CRUST:

2 tablespoons sugar

1 teaspoon table salt

⅔ cup water

1 pound cold unsalted butter, cut into ½-inch dice

4½ cups all-purpose flour, plus more for rolling

FOR THE PIE FILLING:

4 cups rhubarb, chopped

2 quarts fresh strawberries

2 pints fresh blackberries

1 cup light brown sugar

1 cup sugar

⅓ cup cornstarch

2 cups semisweet chocolate chips

1 egg plus 1 tablespoon water, whisked, for egg wash

2 tablespoons Turbinado sugar

Powdered sugar, for garnish

Whipped cream, for garnish

FOR THE PIE CRUST:

1. Preheat oven to 400°F.

2. In a small bowl, dissolve the sugar and salt in the water. Refrigerate until very cold, about 30 minutes. During that time, refrigerate your butter, flour, mixer bowl, and paddle, too.

3. Make sure your butter is cut into ½-inch dice. Bigger pieces will make your dough puffy. In the chilled bowl, combine the cold butter and flour. With your hands, toss the butter in the flour until each cube is lightly coated.

4. With the chilled paddle, beat the flour and butter mixture on low speed to just break up the butter, about 30 seconds. Add the water mixture all at once and raise the speed to medium-low. Beat just until the dough comes together in big chunks, then immediately turn off the mixer.

5. Divide the chunks of dough in half and very gently pat each into a round 1-inch-thick disk. Wrap each tightly in plastic wrap and refrigerate until firm, about 1 hour, before rolling. You can refrigerate the disks for up to 1 day or freeze for up to 3 months.

6. Line the bottom of your oven with a sheet of foil. Grease an 18x13-inch sheet pan.

7. Roll out dough to a 24x19-inch rectangle. Line the pan with 1 piece of dough.

FOR THE PIE FILLING:

8. In a large bowl, combine rhubarb, berries, sugar, and cornstarch. Spread the chocolate chips on the bottom of the pan on top of the dough. Add the berries and top with the remaining dough.

9. In a small bowl, whisk together the egg and 1 tablespoon of water. Brush on top of the dough. Sprinkle with Turbinado sugar.

10. Bake for 35–40 minutes, until top is golden. Serve with powdered sugar and whipped cream.

Pecan Pie Pudding

Serves: 8   **Prep Time:** 5 minutes   **Cook Time:** 30 minutes

I made this dish the last time my dad was on the show because he loves pecan pie, but he hardly ever eats it because it truly is one of the most fattening desserts ever. I wanted him to be able to enjoy his favorite comfort food, so I lightened it up just a bit with this pudding version. Turns out, I was able to **shave off 300 calories** and got the Dr. Oz stamp of approval.

FOR THE VANILLA PUDDING:

¾ cup granulated sugar

⅛ teaspoon salt

⅓ cup all-purpose flour

2 cups milk

2 eggs, separated

2 tablespoons butter, softened

1½ teaspoons vanilla extract

FOR THE CANDIED PECANS:

1 cup chopped pecans

⅓ cup maple syrup

⅓ cup dark brown sugar

¼ teaspoon salt

1 cup graham crackers, coarsely crumbled

FOR THE VANILLA PUDDING:

1. Combine ¾-cup granulated sugar, salt, and flour in a medium bowl. Slowly stir milk into dry mixture. Put mixture in medium saucepot and cook, stirring continuously, until mixture begins to thicken.

2. Beat egg yolks in a small bowl, then briskly stir in a small amount of the hot mixture (about ½ cup), into the eggs. Continue to add the hot mixture into the yolk mixture, whisking continuously, until half of the mixture remains in the pot. Add the yolk mixture back into the pot, stirring continuously. Then add the butter and vanilla and stir to combine. Cook over low heat, stirring continuously with a wooden spoon, until the mixture becomes thick, about 5 minutes. Remove from the heat and set aside.

FOR THE CANDIED PECANS:

3. Toast pecans in a dry nonstick skillet over medium heat for a few minutes. Once toasted, pour in the maple syrup and sprinkle in the sugar. Stir to combine and season with salt. When the sugar has dissolved, remove from heat and allow to cool completely. (This can be made a few days in advance).

TO ASSEMBLE:

4. Place a layer of crumbled graham crackers in the bottom of 8 parfait glasses. Top with a thick layer of pudding and finish with candied pecans. Garnish with additional graham crackers if desired. You can build these parfaits two days in advance and place, covered, in the fridge.

Blackout Cake

Serves: 1   **Prep Time:** 10 minutes   **Cook Time:** 1 hour, 30 minutes

This cake is crazy good. It's the kind of cake that I like to eat curled up on the couch in my pj's with a good movie and a big glass of milk. The combination of cocoa powder and coffee makes the cake batter really dark and incredibly rich. That gets layered with a really silky chocolate frosting, and then it typically gets any of the remaining cake crumbs sprinked on top. But I added a little sea salt instead. Either way, **this cake is comfort food at its best.**

FOR THE CHOCOLATE CRÈME:

2 cups whole milk

2 cups heavy cream

4 large egg yolks

⅓ cup sugar

2 cups (60 percent or higher) dark chocolate, chopped

FOR THE CAKE BATTER:

1¾ cups flour

¾ cup unsweetened cocoa powder (not Dutch-processed)

2 teaspoons baking soda

1 teaspoon baking powder

¾ teaspoon salt

1½ cups sugar

½ cup brown sugar

1 teaspoon instant coffee

1 cup sour cream

⅓ cup water

2 teaspoons vanilla extract

½ cup vegetable oil

3 large eggs

1. Preheat oven to 350°F.

2. Begin by making the chocolate crème. This can be done up to 2 days ahead of time and kept refrigerated.

3. Place your chopped chocolate in a mixing bowl with a strainer set over the top and set aside. Place the milk and cream in a heavy-bottomed saucepot. Bring the mixture up to the point just before boiling. In the meantime, whisk together the egg yolks and sugar in a small mixing bowl until pale and fluffy and no longer grainy. When the milk and cream mixture is up to temp, temper the egg yolks in by slowly whisking in a ladle of the hot cream. Add a few more ladles full, then pour the egg mixture back into the cream mixture. Over medium-low heat, bring the mixture back up to a simmer, while stirring with a rubber spatula. The mixture should thicken slightly. Strain the glaze over your chocolate. Let it sit for a few seconds, allowing the chocolate to begin melting, then whisk everything together until it's a smooth, velvety mixture. Let the crème sit at room temperature until it's no longer steaming, then chill thoroughly until ready to use. It will thicken dramatically as it chills.

FOR THE CAKE BATTER:

4. Preheat your oven to 350°F. Prepare 3 8-inch-round cake pans by lightly spraying the bottoms then fitting with a round of parchment. Once the parchment is in place, butter and flour all of the pans, shaking out all excess.

5. In the bowl of your mixer, sift together the flour, cocoa powder, baking soda, baking powder, and salt.

6. Add both of your sugars and the instant coffee. Using the paddle

FOR THE ICING:

1 bag semisweet chocolate chips

2 sticks unsalted butter, softened

8 ounces cream cheese, softened

2 large egg yolks

1 teaspoon vanilla extract

3 cups powdered sugar, sifted

Pinch of salt

Flaky sea salt, for garnish

separate bowl, whisk together all of the remaining wet ingredients. With the mixer on medium-low speed, add the wet ingredients to the dry ingredients and thoroughly combine. Divide evenly among the 3 pans and place in the oven for 20–25 minutes, until a toothpick inserted in to the center comes out clean. Cool then flip out of the pans and peel the parchment off.

FOR THE ICING:

7. Begin by melting the chocolate chips then setting that aside.

8. In the bowl of your mixer fitted with the whisk attachment, cream the butter and cream cheese together until light and fluffy. Be sure to scrape the sides and bottom of the bowl often to avoid lumps. Next add the egg yolks and vanilla and mix until combined. Next mix in the powdered sugar with a pinch of salt and beat until thoroughly mixed and fluffy. Cover with plastic wrap and set aside until ready to use.

TO ASSEMBLE:

9. Place 1 of the 3 cakes on a plate with the flat side up. Spread a heaping ½ cup of the chocolate crème evenly over the top. Place another cake layer on top with the flat side up. Spread ½ cup of the crème in an even layer, repeating the previous step. Top with the final cake, flat-side up, and gently press down. Place the cake in the freezer for about 10 minutes at this point and it will be easier to frost. Next, frost the cake using the rest of the icing. Sprinkle the top evenly with flaky sea salt. Slice and enjoy!

CLINTON'S "SAVE THE CAKE" TIP
You can keep a cake from drying out once you've cut into it by taking two slices of bread and covering the exposed areas. That way the bread gets stale while your cake stays fresh and moist.

Hot Toddy

Serves: 1   **Prep Time: 1 minute**

Do you ever wonder what to do with that leftover bit of honey at the end of the jar? **Don't throw it away, make a cocktail!** Just pour some bourbon and warm tea right in the glass jar, give it a good shake, and pour into a mug. Garnish with a lemon and you've got yourself a drink that will keep you warm and cozy all winter long.

1 leftover remnant of honey, about 1–2 tablespoons in a jar

4 ounces warm black tea

1 lemon wedge (or a little lemon juice)

1½ ounces bourbon whiskey

1. Pour warm tea and whiskey into a jar of honey. Shake to dissolve honey. Garnish with a squeeze of lemon juice.

2. Serve warm.

HOW TO BUILD A BETTER BURGER

The perfect burger is all about proportion. That patty to bun to condiment ration has to be perfect. I learned this tip for building the perfect burger from my husband Matthew and honey, let me tell you, the outcome is pure bliss! —CARLA HALL

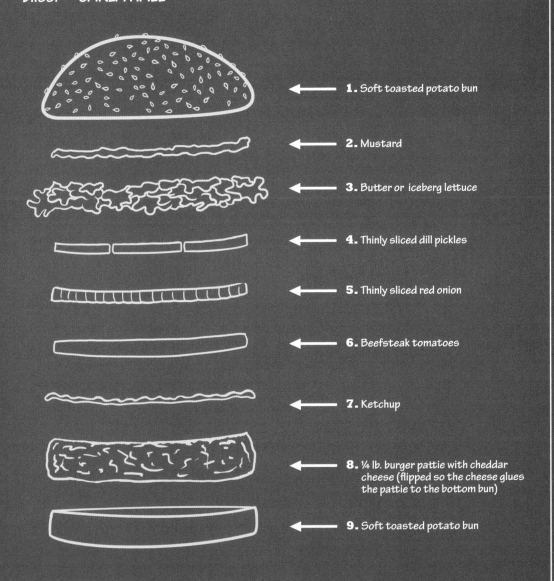

1. Soft toasted potato bun

2. Mustard

3. Butter or iceberg lettuce

4. Thinly sliced dill pickles

5. Thinly sliced red onion

6. Beefsteak tomatoes

7. Ketchup

8. ¼ lb. burger pattie with cheddar cheese (flipped so the cheese glues the pattie to the bottom bun)

9. Soft toasted potato bun

VIEWER Q&A
with CARLA HALL

• •

What is your first cooking memory and your first food memory? —Traci Naumovski, Crystal Lake, IL

Oh, that's easy! The first dish I made was when I was a Girl Scout and I baked an apple crumble for my troop. It was so fun, and I think I did a pretty good job. My first food memory comes from my granny. I was in her house and she was making biscuits. I remember the rolling pin and how there was flour everywhere, and her little tin biscuit cutter that was a little banged up but it just made the most perfect biscuits. I think that's why I'm so obsessed with a perfect biscuit. They always bring me right back to that special time in my childhood.

Carla, you seem like such a positive person. How do you keep that energy? —Shirley Brewer, La Porte, TX

You know life can get very busy, and sometimes, when I'm totally exhausted, I can feel beat down . . . just like everyone else. I think about how lucky I am to have my husband, Matthew, and my family, good friends, and the best job in the world. I mean where else do you get to eat amazing food every day and dance with the audience? I am so blessed!

If you could adopt one of your cohosts, who would it be and why?
—Vicki Tarter, Texarkana, TX

Clinton, of course! If Clinton lived with me, we would spend all day dancing, crafting, [and] cooking, and my wardrobe would be so fabulous. Oh, and the very best part about Clinton is that he would never make a mess. My apartment would be spotless!

FEEL-GOOD

When I was little, my mom would make these giant batches of cookie dough for my birthday parties. Each of the kids got our own big ball to decorate and flavor however we wanted, and then she would bake off these cookie creations and let us dig in. It is still one of my favorite food memories, because she was so great at letting us explore food and be messy and make it our own. It taught me how much fun cooking can be. Moments like that are especially important to me now that I am a mom. Cooking with family, passing down traditions, and coming up with easy recipes that help us spend more time making memories together and less time cleaning up: that's what cooking is all about. So my Chew family and I have passed along some of our favorite family secrets to help your family meals be their best. **—DAPHNE OZ**

FAMILY FAVORITES

Toaster Tarts

Serves: 9   **Prep Time:** 20 minutes   **Cook Time:** 1 hour, 10 minutes

When I was a kid, my mom would let us have one sweet breakfast a week. Pancakes, muffins, sugary cereal, anything we wanted. But my choice was always a toaster tart. Now that I'm a grown up, I like to be able to control the amount of sugar and additives in my food, so I developed this version of one of my childhood favorites. I think **it's better than the original**.

FOR THE STRAWBERRY FILLING:

2 pounds strawberries, hulled

1 cup white sugar, plus more if the berries aren't sweet

1 lemon, zest and juice (about ¼ cup)

2 tablespoons cornstarch

2 teaspoons salt

FOR THE PASTRY:

2 cups all-purpose flour

1 tablespoon granulated sugar

1 teaspoon salt

2 sticks unsalted butter, cut into cubes, chilled

1 large egg

2 tablespoons evaporated milk

1 egg plus 1 tablespoon water, whisked, for egg wash

1 tablespoon cream

FOR THE GLAZE:

1 cup powdered sugar

1 tablespoon water

1 tablespoon sugar

1. Preheat oven to 350°F.

FOR THE STRAWBERRY FILLING:

2. Pulse the strawberries in a food processor until they're the size of peas. Whisk the cornstarch with the lemon juice.

3. In a heavy-bottomed pot, add the strawberries, sugar, lemon zest, cornstarch mixture, and salt. Cook the strawberries over medium-high heat for about 45 minutes, stirring frequently, until the jam is bright red and thick.

4. Let cool before using.

FOR THE PASTRY:

5. Whisk together the flour, sugar, and salt.

6. Work in the butter with your fingers, until pea-size lumps of butter are still visible, and the mixture holds together when you squeeze it.

7. Whisk the egg and evaporated milk together and stir them into the dough, mixing just until everything comes together. Divide the dough in half and shape each half into a smooth rectangle, about 3×5 inches. (This can be kept wrapped in the freezer if you're not using all the dough at once.)

8. Place half the dough on a lightly floured work surface, and roll it out into a large rectangle (about 9x12 inches and about ⅛-inch thick). Repeat with the second piece of dough. Cut each piece of dough into thirds to form 9 3x4-inch rectangles.

9. Beat the additional egg and cream and brush it over the half of the rectangles. This will be the "inside" of the tart; the egg is to help glue the top on.

10. Place a heaping tablespoon of strawberry filling into the center of each rectangle, keeping the ½-inch perimeter around it free of filling. Place a second rectangle of dough atop the first, using your fingertips to press firmly around the pocket of filling, sealing the dough well on all sides. Use the tines of a fork to crimp the edges. Brush tops with the egg wash. Repeat with remaining tarts.

11. Gently place the tarts on a parchment-lined baking sheet. Prick the top of each tart multiple times with a fork. Refrigerate the tarts (they don't need to be covered) for 30 minutes.

12. Remove the tarts from the fridge, and bake them for 20–25 minutes, until they are a light golden brown.

13. Cool on a rack.

14. Combine confectioners' sugar, lemon juice, and water. Drizzle over tarts, then serve.

The Chew: An Essential Guide to Cooking and Entertaining

Waffle Iron Croissant Sandwich

Serves: 2   **Prep Time:** *5 minutes*   **Cook Time:** *5 minutes*

I know how crazy the morning routine can feel when you're trying to get the kids fed and ready for school (and you're trying to get ready for work). It can be a little overwhelming at times. So I'm always trying to figure out ways to make things a little bit easier on myself during that morning shuffle. **I had a real lightbulb moment** when I realized that I could make perfectly cooked eggs sandwiches in the waffle maker in just around five minutes. These sandwiches will make the whole family happy, especially you.

1 croissant, sliced in half

4 eggs, whisked

¼ pound sliced bacon, cooked and crumbled

½ cup shredded cheddar cheese

2 scallions, thinly sliced

Salt and freshly ground black pepper, to taste

Nonstick cooking spray

1. Preheat a waffle iron to medium. Spray both sides of the iron with cooking spray.

2. In a medium bowl, whisk together eggs, bacon, cheddar, and scallions. Season with salt and pepper. Divide half the egg mixture into 2 squares of the waffle iron. Place both halves of the croissant into 2 of the remaining waffle squares. Close and cook for 2 minutes. Remove all items from the waffle iron. Place egg waffle on half of the croissant. Top with the remaining half croissant.

French Toast Sticks

Serves: 8   Prep Time: 5 minutes   Cook Time: 10 minutes

I make this dish sometimes when I throw a brunch at my house for friends because it turns French toast into finger food, and it's an interesting addition to a buffet table. I also find that kids, especially, **love dunking the French toast** into little cups of maple syrup. These are so fun and playful that you'll want to make them every weekend.

8 slices brioche, preferably day-old, cut into 1x3-inch sticks

4 eggs

½ cup milk

½ cup half-and-half

¼ cup maple syrup, plus more for serving

½ teaspoon cinnamon

Pinch of salt

2 tablespoons butter

¼ cup brown sugar

Powdered sugar

1. Preheat oven to broil. In a large bowl, whisk eggs, milk, half-and-half, maple syrup, cinnamon, and a pinch of salt.

2. Place breadsticks in a 9x13-inch baking dish. Pour the custard mixture over the bread, allowing bread to soak up the custard but not get too soggy, only a minute or two.

3. Heat a large oven-safe nonstick sauté pan over medium heat. Add the butter and allow it to melt. Take the French toast sticks and place them in an even layer in the pan. Cook for 2–3 minutes per side, allowing them to brown.

4. With the French toast sticks still in the pan, sprinkle brown sugar evenly over the top. Place in the oven and allow sugar to caramelize, about 2 minutes.

5. Serve warm with maple syrup for dipping and powdered sugar.

Lunch Box Yogurt Parfait

Serves: 1   Prep Time: 10 minutes

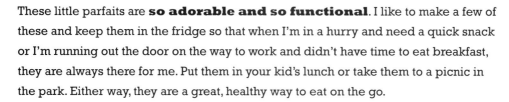

These little parfaits are **so adorable and so functional**. I like to make a few of these and keep them in the fridge so that when I'm in a hurry and need a quick snack or I'm running out the door on the way to work and didn't have time to eat breakfast, they are always there for me. Put them in your kid's lunch or take them to a picnic in the park. Either way, they are a great, healthy way to eat on the go.

½ cup Greek yogurt

¼ cup blueberries

¼ cup granola

1 tablespoon honey

In an 8-ounce jar with a lid, layer yogurt, berries, and granola. Top with honey to desired sweetness and cover with lid if not serving immediately.

The Chew team takes a selfie with Daphne's husband, John, and their daughter, Philo.

The Chew: An Essential Guide to Cooking and Entertaining

Caramelized Onion and Sausage Puffs

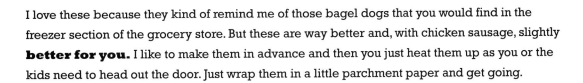

Serves: 8   Prep Time: 5 minutes   Cook Time: 15 minutes

I love these because they kind of remind me of those bagel dogs that you would find in the freezer section of the grocery store. But these are way better and, with chicken sausage, slightly **better for you.** I like to make them in advance and then you just heat them up as you or the kids need to head out the door. Just wrap them in a little parchment paper and get going.

2 large yellow onions

2 tablespoons olive oil

2 tablespoons unsalted butter

1 sheet store-bought puff pastry, thawed

1 egg + 1 tablespoon water, whisked

4 chicken apple sausage links, halved lengthwise

Poppy seeds, to garnish

Salt, to taste

1. Preheat oven to 400°F. Line a baking sheet with parchment and set aside.

2. Heat a large skillet over medium with olive oil and butter. Once the butter melts, add the sliced onions and season with salt. Cook the onions, stirring occasionally, until caramelized, about 15–20 minutes. Remove from heat and allow to cool.

3. Lay the puff pastry on a lightly floured surface and cut into 8 rectangles the length of the sausage.

4. Divide the caramelized onions between the 8 pieces of pastry dough. Lay a sausage link on top. Wrap the dough around the sausage to completely enclose. Gently press the dough to seal.

5. Transfer the wrapped sausages to the prepared baking sheet, brush each with the egg wash, and sprinkle with salt and poppy seeds. Bake for 12–15 minutes or until the pastry is puffed and golden.

6. Remove from oven and serve warm as a fun on-the-go breakfast.

Banana Dippers

These are not only a fun snack for kids to eat, but they are a great way to get the kids in the kitchen and a great project to keep them entertained. The flavor combinations are endless and this recipe really allows everyone to get creative. I like to have these on hand in the freezer because they are such **a wonderful alternative** to other sugary frozen treats.

FOR THE PEANUT BUTTER COVERED BANANAS:

1 cup dark chocolate, chopped

5 tablespoons creamy peanut butter

3 bananas, cut in half crosswise

TOPPINGS:

Chopped peanuts

Coconut flakes

Chopped almonds

SPECIAL EQUIPMENT:

Popsicle sticks

1. Peel and freeze bananas for 2 hours and up to overnight.

2. Over a double boiler, melt together chocolate and peanut butter. Insert Popsicle sticks into the frozen bananas. Dip bananas in chocolate and peanut butter mixture. Roll in desired toppings. Put dipped bananas on wax paper and freeze until set, about 30 minutes.

Pizza Rolls

Serves: 8-10   Prep Time: 15 minutes   Cook Time: 30 minutes

Growing up in a Greek and Sicilian family, I had parents who never sent me to school with a turkey sandwich and chips. It was more like lasagna and leftover lamb sandwiches. But on occasion, I would open my lunch box to find that my dad had packed pizza rolls. These little wheels of pepperoni and cheese were my favorite. And let me tell you, on pizza roll day, I was **the most popular kid in school!**

1 pound store-bought pizza dough

¼ cup store-bought tomato sauce

4 cups fresh mozzarella, grated

Salt and freshly ground black pepper, to taste

5 tablespoons fresh Parmesan, plus more for garnish

½ pound sliced pepperoni

1 bunch fresh basil

Olive oil

Chili flakes for garnish

1. Preheat oven to 375°F.

2. On a lightly floured surface, roll out the pizza dough into a 10x11-inch rectangle. Spread 3 tablespoons of sauce over the entire surface, leaving about a 1-inch border. Spread out about ½ cup of the grated mozzarella over the sauce and season lightly with salt and freshly ground black pepper. Sprinkle about 2 teaspoons of Parmesan over the top of this. Next start layering the pepperoni on top, 16–20 slices, then place 5 or 6 whole basil leaves in a horizontal line in the center of the pizza. Drizzle a little bit of olive oil over the whole pizza.

3. Working with the side closest to you, roll the pizza up, pinching the seam, and then tuck each side under. Place on a lightly oiled parchment-lined sheet tray. Drizzle some olive oil on top of the pizza roll, then crack some pepper on top and sprinkle a little bit of the chili flakes and Parmesan over the top. Makes 3 slits in the top of each roll.

4. Bake for 20–30 minutes, or until the top is very golden brown, making sure the dough in the center is not raw. Remove from the oven and let rest for about 5 minutes before slicing.

Mario's Spicy Dollar-Saving Pasta

Serves: 4   Prep Time: *10 minutes*   **Cook Time:** *10 minutes*

When you're cooking for your family, it's always nice to know that there are delicious meals that you can make that cost very little money. Obviously, for me, pasta is the way to go because that's the place that you can really **stretch your dollar the most.** I always look to my pantry to find those flavor boosters, like onions, garlic, and tomato paste, to really build layers of flavor that make any pasta dish taste like a million bucks!

1 pound spaghettini

1 yellow onion, sliced

2 garlic cloves, sliced

1 bunch scallions, chopped, green parts reserved

½ pound Italian sausage, cut into 1-inch pieces

¼ cup tomato paste

4 jalapeños

FOR THE BREAD-CRUMB TOPPING:

1 cup panko bread crumbs

¼ cup extra-virgin olive oil, divided

1. Bring a large pot of salted water to a boil. Add the pasta and cook until al dente. Drain, reserving some of the pasta liquid.

2. Meanwhile, preheat a large sauté pan over medium-high heat. Add a drizzle of olive oil. Once hot, add the onions, garlic, and scallions, and season with salt and pepper. Cook until translucent, about 2 minutes. Then add the sausage and cook until the sausage is caramelized and cooked through, about 5 minutes. Add the tomato paste and half of the jalapeños. Cook for 2 more minutes.

3. Add the drained pasta and a ladle of pasta water. Stir to combine. Add more pasta water if necessary to loosen and create a sauce. Garnish with bread-crumb topping and more sliced jalapeños. Drizzle with extra-virgin olive oil.

FOR THE BREAD-CRUMB TOPPING:

4. Preheat a large nonstick sauté pan over medium heat. Add the bread crumbs to a dry pan and stir until golden brown. Then add a drizzle of olive oil and the reserved scallion greens. Sauté for one more minute. Remove from heat and set aside.

Daphne's Turkey Tacos with Creamy Chipotle Dressing

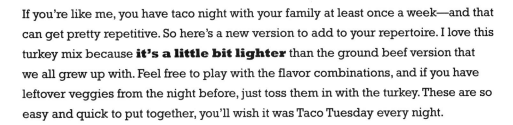

Serves: 12   Prep Time: 15 minutes   Cook Time: 15 minutes

If you're like me, you have taco night with your family at least once a week—and that can get pretty repetitive. So here's a new version to add to your repertoire. I love this turkey mix because **it's a little bit lighter** than the ground beef version that we all grew up with. Feel free to play with the flavor combinations, and if you have leftover veggies from the night before, just toss them in with the turkey. These are so easy and quick to put together, you'll wish it was Taco Tuesday every night.

FOR THE TACOS:

2 tablespoons olive oil

2 pounds ground turkey

1 tablespoon ground cumin

1 tablespoon chipotle chili powder

Salt and freshly ground black pepper, to taste

1 onion, diced

2 cloves garlic, minced

1 jalapeño, seeded and minced

2 tablespoons tomato paste

1 can pinto beans, drained

12 hard taco shells

FOR THE SHREDDED SALAD:

1 red onion, diced

1 head romaine, shredded

1 tomato, diced

1 cup green pimento-stuffed olives, sliced

FOR THE CREAMY CHIPOTLE DRESSING:

1 cup vegan mayonnaise

1 teaspoon chipotle chili powder

1 teaspoon honey

Juice of 2 limes

2 tablespoons apple-cider vinegar

Pinch of salt

1. Heat a large skillet over medium-high heat and add the oil and the ground turkey. Cook until it begins to brown, about 5 minutes, and then add the onion, garlic, and jalapeño pepper, and cook for another 3 minutes. Stir in the spices and tomato paste and season with salt and pepper to taste. Continue cooking until liquid has reduced slightly. Add pinto beans and stir to combine.

2. Combine all of the ingredients for the salad in a large bowl and set aside.

3. To make the dressing, whisk together all of the ingredients and add a pinch of salt. Pour over the salad ingredients and toss to coat. Serve with the tacos.

4. To assemble, fill a taco shell with the turkey mixture and top with the salad.

Batali Beef and Barley Soup

Serves: 6   Prep Time: 15 minutes   Cook Time: 3 hours, 30 minutes

When I was a kid, my mom used to make soup once a week, and this one was by far my favorite. This soup would sit on the stove for hours and fill the house with the most joyous aromas. Just before my mom would serve it up, she would crack one egg for each of us into the pot. The eggs would poach to perfection. And I still remember how excited I was to cut into it and watch the yolk pour out into the bowl. My mouth is watering just thinking about it now. **Love you, Mom!**

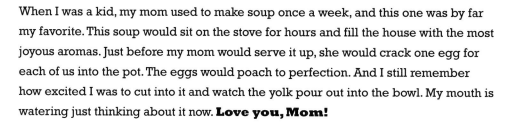

3 pounds beef chuck, cut into 1½-inch cubes

Salt and freshly ground black pepper, to taste

1 yellow onion, chopped

1 cup carrot, sliced into half-moons, ½-inch thick

1 cup celery, ½-inch slice

1 jalapeño, sliced

2 tablespoons tomato paste

1 small bunch thyme

2 dried bay leaves

10 cups beef stock

1 cup barley

6 eggs

3 tablespoons chopped parsley, to garnish

Hot sauce, optional

1. Preheat a large heavy-bottomed pot or Dutch oven over medium-high heat. Add a drizzle of oil. Once hot, add half of the beef and season with salt and pepper. Sear the beef until browned on all sides. Remove beef to a plate with a slotted spoon and set aside. Add the rest of the meat and repeat process. Add the onions, carrots, celery, and jalapeño, season with salt and pepper and sauté for 5 minutes, or until translucent. Add the tomato paste, stir to coat and cook for 2 minutes. Add the beef back into the pot, along with the thyme, bay leaves, and beef stock. Bring to a boil. Reduce heat to a simmer, cover, and cook on low heat, stirring occasionally, for 2 hours.

2. At this point, add the barley. Cook for another hour.

3. When the barley is tender, carefully crack a few eggs on top of the stew. Cover with a lid and cook until the whites of the eggs have set, about 8 minutes.

4. Serve a bowl of soup with a poached egg in the center of it. Garnish with chopped parsley and a few dashes of hot sauce if desired.

Dad's Hot Dog Hash

Serves: 4   Prep Time: 5 minutes   Cook Time: 5 minutes

This dish is **one of my all-time favorite childhood dishes!** It's not gourmet by any stretch of the imagination, but it's still so special to me. My dad used to work the graveyard shift when I was a kid and his only day off was Sunday. So on Sunday mornings my sister and I would run downstairs to find a big pan of this stuff waiting for us. It was the best day of the week, and I can still remember how sweet it was to eat it together as a family.

2 tablespoons olive oil

4 medium Idaho potatoes, skin-on, small dice

1 small package of yellow onions, sliced thinly

4 hot dogs, sliced into coins

Salt and freshly ground black pepper, to taste

1 tablespoon butter

4 large eggs

Hot sauce, to serve

1. Heat 2 large sauté pans over medium-high heat. To one pan, add the olive oil, along with the potatoes, keeping them in an even layer. Cook the potatoes until they start to turn golden brown, about 2 minutes, then mix them and move them around a bit. Add the onion and hot dogs to the potatoes and gently mix to combine. Season with salt and freshly ground black pepper and continue cooking over medium-high heat until everything starts to caramelize, another 3 minutes.

2. While the hash is finishing up, add the butter to the second pan. When the butter has melted and coated the bottom of the pan, add all four eggs. Cook the eggs until the whites are set and the yolk is still runny, about 2 minutes. Baste the eggs with butter as they cook. Season them with salt and pepper; then turn the heat off.

3. Spoon some of the hot dog hash onto a plate and top with a fried egg.

Baked Lasagna alla Norma

Serves: 8–10   **Prep Time:** 30 minutes   **Cook Time:** 1 hour, 10 minutes

This is **my twist on the classic eggplant pasta** dish named after the Italian opera. Here I turned it into lasagna for our good friend Robin Roberts from *Good Morning America*, who is just like family to us and has been stopping by the show for years. This dish is one of her favorites, and I guarantee that once you make it at home, it will quickly become part of your weekly dinner rotation.

FOR THE EGGPLANT-TOMATO SAUCE:

3 tablespoons extra-virgin olive oil, plus more for the pan

2 medium eggplants, peeled and cut into medium dice

1 medium red onion, cut into ¼-inch dice

2 cloves garlic, thinly sliced

2 28-ounce cans Italian plum tomatoes, crushed by hand, juices reserved

3 tablespoons chopped fresh basil, about 2 large sprigs

1 tablespoon fresh thyme leaves

Salt and freshly ground black pepper, to taste

FOR THE BÉCHAMEL:

5 tablespoons unsalted butter

¼ cup all-purpose flour

3 cups whole milk

2 teaspoons kosher salt

½ teaspoon freshly grated nutmeg

TO ASSEMBLE:

2 tablespoons kosher salt

1 1-pound package lasagna noodles

1 cup freshly grated Parmesan

4 tablespoons ricotta salata, grated to serve

FOR THE EGGPLANT-TOMATO SAUCE:

1. Preheat oven to 475°F. Lightly oil a baking sheet.

2. Place the eggplant on the preheated baking sheet and roast until soft and dark golden brown, 15–20 minutes. Remove and allow to cool. Reduce the oven temperature to 375°F.

3. While the eggplant is roasting, heat the 3 tablespoons of olive oil in a 12–14-inch sauté pan until smoking. Add the onion and garlic and cook until soft and light golden brown, 5–6 minutes. Add the tomatoes, basil, and thyme, and bring to a boil. Simmer for 15 minutes, and season with salt and pepper. Add the cooked eggplant cubes and simmer for 6 minutes. Remove from the heat and set aside.

FOR THE BÉCHAMEL:

4. In a medium saucepan, melt the butter over medium heat. Add the flour and stir until smooth. Cook until light golden brown, about 5 minutes. Add the milk, 1 cup at a time, whisking continuously until smooth. Bring to a boil and cook for 5 minutes, season with salt and nutmeg, and set aside.

TO ASSEMBLE:

5. Bring 8 quarts of water to a boil in a pasta pot and add the salt. Set up an ice bath next to the stove top. Drop the pasta into the boiling water, 6 or 7 pieces at a time, and cook about 5 minutes less than suggested on the package. Transfer to the ice bath to cool, then drain on kitchen towels, laying the pasta flat. Repeat to cook the rest of the pasta.

6. Spread a layer of the eggplant-tomato sauce over the bottom of a 9x13-inch lasagna pan and top with a sprinkling of Parmesan, a layer of pasta, a layer of béchamel, another layer of eggplant-tomato sauce, a sprinkling of Parmesan, and a layer of pasta. Repeat until all ingredients are used up, finishing with a layer of pasta topped with béchamel and a sprinkling of Parmesan.

7. Bake for 45 minutes, or until the edges are browned and the sauces are bubbling around the edges of the pan. Let stand for 10 minutes before serving.

8. Serve with ricotta salata grated over the top and extra sauce if desired.

CLINTON'S "PLACE CARD" TIP

Did you know that you can make place cards out of pasta? I like to buy the alphabet shapes and glue the names of my guests onto each card. It's a fun way to experiment with seating arrangements at a dinner party.

Sheet Pan Chicken Thighs with Fingerling Potatoes

Serves: 4   **Prep Time:** *10 minutes*   **Cook Time:** *45 minutes*

With a little kid running around the house, it's hard for me to stand around the stove all night. So passive cooking is really something that I've been doing a lot lately. And for that, the sheet pan has become my secret weapon for getting dinner on the table with as little mess and fuss as possible. **This dish is so easy**, you literally toss everything together in a bowl with some olive oil, spread it out evenly on the sheet pan, and bake it for about 45 minutes. In the end, you've got a healthy and incredibly flavorful dinner ready to go in no time.

8 chicken thighs, boneless, skinless

1 bulb fennel, sliced into 1-inch slices, fronds chopped and reserved

1 onion, sliced into ½-inch slices

1 pound fingerling potatoes, halved

2 teaspoons garlic powder

1 lemon, zest and juice

2 teaspoons salt

Freshly ground black pepper

2 tablespoons extra-virgin olive oil

1. Preheat oven to 400°F.

2. To a large bowl, add chicken, fennel, onion, potatoes, garlic powder, lemon juice, and zest. Toss with salt, pepper, olive oil, and remaining chopped fennel fronds until well coated. Spread onto a large baking sheet, piling the vegetables up around the sides and the chicken in the center of the pan.

3. Roast for 45 minutes to an hour until chicken is cooked through and vegetables are soft and caramelized.

CARLA'S "NO MESS" TIP

If you really want to avoid a mess, just cover the sheet pan with foil, and when you plate the chicken just throw that foil in the recycling. No soaking or scrubbing required.

Mrs. Batali's Chicken Cacciatore

Serves: 4   Prep Time: 20 minutes   Cook Time: 45 minutes

This is not the traditional preparation of chicken cacciatore, but it's the way my mom made it—and I love it. The shiitake mushrooms and leeks bring an earthiness to the dish that takes me back to her kitchen every time I eat it. It's become a classic in my house, and once you try this version you're sure to crave it just as much as I do. **It's just that good.**

2 tablespoons extra-virgin olive oil

¼ pound pancetta, ½-inch dice

1 pound shiitake mushrooms, sliced

3–4 pound chicken, cut into 8 pieces

Salt and freshly ground black pepper, to taste

1 red onion, sliced

3 cloves garlic, chopped

2 red bell peppers, ¼-inch dice

2 leeks, cleaned and cut into ½-inch moons

Pinch of red pepper flakes

3 sprigs rosemary

1 cup dry Italian white wine, such as pinot grigio

1½ cups chicken stock

2 bay leaves

1 bunch basil, leaves torn

1. Preheat a large heavy-bottomed pot or Dutch oven over medium heat. Add the olive oil and pancetta. Cook until browned and crispy. Push aside in the pot. Add the mushrooms and sauté until well browned. Remove the pancetta and mushrooms from the pot and set aside.

2. Meanwhile, pat the chicken dry. Season on all sides with salt and pepper. Place the chicken skin-side down in the pot. After about 4 minutes, when well browned, flip all the chicken and brown well on the other side. Remove the chicken from the pot and set aside.

3. Remove excess grease if necessary. Add the onions, garlic, peppers, leeks, red pepper flakes, and rosemary and season with salt and pepper. Sauté over medium-high heat until translucent and slightly caramelized, about 6 minutes. Add the wine and use a wooden spoon to scrape the brown bits from the bottom of the pan. Add the stock and bring to a simmer. Then add the reserved chicken and bay leaves. Lay the chicken in the sauce skin-side up. Bring to a simmer, then reduce the heat to low. Let cook for 30 minutes until tender.

4. Add the reserved pancetta and mushrooms, as well as the basil, into the sauce. Remove from heat and serve.

Hazelnut Hot Chocolate

Serves: 1   Prep Time: 1 minute

One of America's **favorite tasty temptations** is chocolate-hazelnut spread. You know how sad it can be to get to the bottom of that jar, so I developed this recipe to turn the saddest day into the best day of your life. Just pour a little warm milk in there with some cinnamon and vanilla, put the top back on, and shake it like you mean it! It's so good I can't ever wait to pour it into a glass; I just drink it straight from the jar.

1–2 tablespoons leftover chocolate-hazelnut spread (in the bottom of the jar)

1 cup warm milk

¼ teaspoon vanilla extract

Pinch of ground cinnamon

1. Add the warm milk, vanilla extract, and cinnamon to the jar of leftover chocolate-hazelnut spread.

2. Shake well to combine. Pour in a mug or drink directly from the jar.

DAPHNE'S "NON-SLIP" TIP
I know that Philo sometimes has a hard time keeping her cup from slipping out of her hands, so here's a great tip to keep that drink from landing all over your new rug, Just tie a rubber band around the middle of the cup. It gives the glass the traction and grip needed to stay in your little one's hands.

Apple Cake with Cream Cheese Frosting

Serves: 10   Prep Time: 40 minutes   Cook Time: 50 minutes

This cake is really great for younger kids because it is not supersweet, and a lot of the ingredients are things that they already eat, like apples, yogurt, and oranges. I made this cake with Daphne for her daughter Philo's first birthday. And let's face it, when you make a cake for a one-year-old, you know they're gonna get more of it on their face and clothes than in their mouth anyway. Judging by the mess, **I think Philo loved it!**

FOR THE CAKE:

3 cups cake flour

1 cup light brown sugar

1 tablespoon baking powder

1 teaspoon salt

4 tablespoons butter, softened to room temperature

½ cup canola oil

3 large eggs, at room temperature

½ cup applesauce, at room temperature

2 teaspoons vanilla extract

½ cup yogurt, at room temperature

FOR THE COMPOTE:

2 tablespoons butter

3 apples, diced

¼ cup light brown sugar

½ cup orange juice

½ teaspoon cinnamon

FOR THE CREAM CHEESE FROSTING:

2 8-ounce packages cream cheese, softened

1 stick butter, softened

1½ cups powdered sugar

1 teaspoon vanilla extract

FOR THE CAKE:

1. Preheat oven to 350°F. Prepare 3 9-inch cake pans by coating with butter, lining with a round of parchment, coating that with butter, and dusting with flour.

2. It is important that all the ingredients are at room temperature.

3. In a large mixing bowl, combine flour, light brown sugar, baking powder, and salt.

4. Add butter and canola oil.

5. In a medium bowl, combine eggs, applesauce, and vanilla. Add to the flour mixture. Stir in the yogurt just to incorporate.

6. Divide the batter between the 3 cake pans and bake 15–20 minutes, until cake is golden brown and pulls away from the pan. Cool for 10 minutes, then remove from pan and transfer to a rack to cool completely.

FOR THE COMPOTE:

7. In a small saucepan over medium-high heat, combine butter, apples, brown sugar, orange juice, and cinnamon. Simmer 15 minutes until thickened and apples are soft.

FOR THE CREAM CHEESE FROSTING:

8. Beat cream cheese and butter until creamy and smooth. Slowly add the powdered sugar until well incorporated. Beat in vanilla.

The Chew: An Essential Guide to Cooking and Entertaining

TO ASSEMBLE THE CAKE:

9. Using a serrated knife, trim the tops of the cakes to make them even. Spread half of the compote mixture on the first cake. Place the second cake on top and repeat with remaining compote. Place the final cake on top. Frost the top and sides with a thin layer and refrigerate for 20 minutes. Complete with remaining frosting over chilled cake.

CLINTON'S "LAUNDRY" TIP

Kids can be messy. Want some help keeping their clothes tidy? Add a pinch or two of salt to your wash to keep colors from fading. And did you know that you can loosely crumple a piece of tinfoil and use it in place of dryer sheets? It's great for people with sensitive skin. Amazing, I know.

Dad's Death by Chocolate

Serves: 10   **Prep Time:** 2 hours, 30 minutes   **Cook Time:** 5 minutes

At every holiday party, we would look forward to my dad's Death by Chocolate. And to this day, it is still **one of my favorite desserts.** One day I called him up asking for the recipe because I wanted to put it on the menu at one of my restaurants (it's that good)—and he told me it's just a couple of packets of instant chocolate pudding, whipped cream, and some chocolate candy sprinkled on top. Well, I couldn't put that on a restaurant menu, so I came up with this homemade version.

1 quart heavy cream

¼ cup powdered sugar

½ cup crème fraîche

Chocolate pudding (below)

3 cups crumbled chocolate wafer cookies

4¼ ounces chocolate-covered English toffee bars, chopped

FOR THE CHOCOLATE PUDDING:

4 egg yolks

1½ cups sugar

1 quart heavy cream

1 teaspoon salt

1 cup unsweetened cocoa

⅓ cup all-purpose flour

1 stick butter, cubed

1 cup bittersweet chocolate chips

1. In a large bowl, whip the heavy cream with the powdered sugar until soft peaks start to form, about 5 minutes. Gently fold in the crème fraîche.

2. In a large trifle bowl, place a thick layer of the chocolate pudding, top with a layer of the whipped cream mixture, and then sprinkle on half of the cookies and half of the toffee candy. Repeat the process, finishing with the cookies and candy on top. Cover with plastic wrap. Chill for 2 hours and serve.

FOR THE CHOCOLATE PUDDING:

3. Whisk the egg yolks and sugar together in a medium bowl. Add the cream and salt and whisk until combined. Mix the cocoa and flour together, and then whisk the wet ingredients into the dry. Place the mixture in a heavy saucepan over medium heat and stir continuously until the mixture comes to a simmer, about 5 minutes. Remove from heat and stir in the butter and chocolate until melted. Let cool.

Granny's Five-Flavor Pound Cake

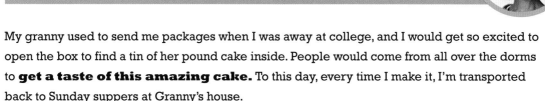

Serves: 12   Prep Time: 15 minutes   Cook Time: 1 hour

My granny used to send me packages when I was away at college, and I would get so excited to open the box to find a tin of her pound cake inside. People would come from all over the dorms to **get a taste of this amazing cake.** To this day, every time I make it, I'm transported back to Sunday suppers at Granny's house.

Nonstick baking spray

3 cups all-purpose flour

1 teaspoon baking soda

1 teaspoon salt

8 tablespoons unsalted butter, cut into tablespoons, at room temperature

2½ cups sugar

6 large eggs, at room temperature

1 cup sour cream, at room temperature

1 teaspoon vanilla extract

1 teaspoon rum extract

1 teaspoon coconut extract

1 teaspoon lemon extract

1 teaspoon almond extract

SPECIAL EQUIPMENT:

10-cup bundt pan or tube pan

1. Spray a 10-cup bundt or tube pan with nonstick cooking spray.

2. Sift the flour into a large bowl. Add the baking soda and salt and stir to combine.

3. In the bowl of an electric mixer fitted with a paddle, cream the butter and sugar on medium-high speed until pale and fluffy, about 3 minutes. Stop and scrape down the sides and bottom of the bowl. With the mixer on medium, add the eggs one at a time, completely incorporating each egg before adding the next. Stop and scrape down the bowl.

4. With the mixer on low speed, add the flour in thirds, alternating with the sour cream and beginning and ending with the flour. Continue beating for 2 minutes on medium speed, stopping to scrape the sides and bottom of the bowl occasionally. Add the extracts one at a time, completely incorporating each before adding the next. Continue beating until the batter is shiny, about 4 minutes.

5. Pour the batter into the cake pan. Turn the oven to 300°F and place cake in the cool oven. Bake until the cake is golden and a toothpick inserted in the center comes out clean, about 1 hour, 20 minutes.

6. Let the cake cook in the pan on a wire rack for 10 minutes, then unmold onto the rack. Let the cake cool completely.

7. The cake will keep in an airtight container for up to a week.

Mom's Greek Cookies

Serves: 85   **Prep Time:** 5 minutes   **Cook Time:** 1 hour, 20 minutes

When I was about seven or eight, I remember walking into my mom's kitchen around the holidays and seeing all my aunts and my *yaya* making a ton of these cookies for Christmas. It would be a full-on production because they would give them out as gifts for family and friends. Everyone at *The Chew* can attest to **how amazing these cookies are** since my mom sends about a thousand to the studio every year for the whole crew to enjoy.

3 sticks unsalted butter, softened

1½ cups granulated sugar

3 egg yolks (reserving the whites)

1 egg

8 ounces heavy cream

1 teaspoon vanilla

1 box cake flour

2½ teaspoons baking powder

White sesame seeds

1. In the bowl of your mixer fitted with the paddle attachment, cream the butter and sugar until light and fluffy. Next add the egg yolks and egg and mix until just incorporated before slowly adding the cream and vanilla.

2. Mix together the flour and baking powder, then add it to the butter mixture. Mix until the dough comes together, scraping down the sides throughout this process.

3. Chill the dough for at least 30 minutes or until ready to use.

4. Preheat oven to 350°F. Whip the reserved egg whites until light and frothy. Set aside.

5. To shape the cookies, pinch off a piece of dough about the size of a walnut. Roll out a cord or thin tube of dough about the length of a dinner knife. Fold in half then twist two times. Pinch the remaining edges together and tuck underneath.

6. Place on a parchment-lined baking sheet while you form the rest.

7. When all of the cookies are formed, brush them with the reserved egg whites and sprinkle with a little bit of sesame seeds. Bake for about 20 minutes, or until light golden brown. Cool completely before storing in an airtight container, or form them into braids and freeze the dough.

DAPHNE'S "REMOVAL" TIP
Ever wonder how to get crayon off of your walls? Well, it's easy: just take about 4 tablespoons of vegetable oil and mix in 2 tablespoons of baking soda. Add a little of the mixture to a dry towel and the crayon comes right off, leaving you feeling like a supermom in no time.

Blackberry Roly-Poly

Serves: 8　　**Prep Time:** 10 minutes　　**Cook Time:** 50 minutes

We get letters all the time from our viewers asking for help in the kitchen. This recipe came from an eighty-five-year-old southern viewer who wanted to make her grandmother's blackberry roly-poly but couldn't find the recipe. No one in her family remembered how to make it, either. I had never heard of a roly-poly, so I did some research and we tested some ideas in *The Chew* kitchen. As a result, we came up with this really delicious version. And when the viewer tried it, she said it tasted just like she remembered. **Problem solved!**

1 tablespoon butter for greasing

1¼ cups self-rising flour, plus more for dusting

2 tablespoons granulated sugar

½ teaspoon salt

⅓ cup vegetable shortening

⅓ cup milk

½ cup blackberry jam

Greek yogurt or heavy cream to serve

FOR THE BLACKBERRY JAM:

3 cups fresh blackberries, crushed

1 ounce powdered pectin

3½ cups granulated sugar

1 lemon, juice and zest, plus more to garnish

1. Preheat oven to 400°F.

2. Grease a 9x13 piece of parchment paper with butter.

3. Whisk together the flour, sugar, and salt in a large bowl.

4. Work in the vegetable shortening until crumbly.

5. Stir in milk with a wooden spoon until almost completely incorporated.

6. Roll out dough on a lightly floured surface to form a rectangle about ¼-inch thick.

7. Spread the jam across the surface of the dough leaving a 1-inch border.

8. Roll the dough widthwise and seal the edge with your fingers.

9. Place the roll seam-side down in the center of the greased parchment. Wrap the roll in the parchment making sure not to wrap it too tight. Twist the edges to seal. Wrap the entire package loosely in foil.

10. Place the wrapped package on a rack set inside a baking sheet. Place the baking sheet in the oven and pour hot water in the pan making sure the water does not touch the foil.

11. Bake for 45 minutes.

12. Carefully remove from the oven and gently pull back the foil and parchment.

13. Allow to cool slightly before slicing and serving each with lemon zest, plus a dollop of Greek yogurt or a splash of cream.

FOR THE BLACKBERRY JAM:

14. Combine the fruit, sugar, and pectin. Bring to a boil in a large saucepot, stirring to dissolve the sugar. Boil, stirring constantly, for about 2 minutes. Transfer to a jar or bowl and allow to cool completely.

HOMEMADE SIDEWALK CHALK

Whether it's in the park or at the playground, when summer rolls around my family and I are always outside. So I always have with me a huge bag filled with sand toys, bubbles, and of course sidewalk chalk. This DIY, family friendly trick for making chalk at home is as easy to create, as it is to use. Your family will love it! —DAPHNE OZ

1. Buy Plaster of Paris at just about any hardware store.

2. Stir about 3 parts Plaster of Paris into 1 part warm water until it is the consistency of thick pancake batter.

3. Stir in your favorite color of finger paint or washable tempera paint. Definitely experiment with swirls and color combinations.

4. Cover one end of a paper towel or toilet paper roll with wax paper and secure with a rubber band.

5. Spoon the colored plaster into the roll and let sit overnight.

6. Remove the roll by peeling it from the hardened plaster and send the kids to the driveway.

VIEWER Q&A

with DAPHNE OZ

If you had to choose to be more like one of your cohosts, who would it be and why? —Jessie Bizenov, Princeton, NJ

There are qualities in each of my cohosts that I appreciate and admire. Mario has an incredible memory, and is super-passionate about everything he does. Clinton is so witty, and is one of the most charming and gracious people I've ever met. Carla has this amazing ability to be herself in any situation, and she enjoys life no matter what it brings her. And Michael has such a big heart and a great sense of humor. I don't want to be like any of them—I just want to keep them all!

What part of your life has changed the most since becoming a mother? —Melissa Olsen, North Brunswick, NJ

My priorities changed the second I had a baby. Your time is never your own again, and that's OK. I think that learning that you don't have to be perfect and that for the most part there is no "right way" to do things was a really important lesson for me as a new mom.

If you could have any job, what would it be?
—Nicholas Mallas, Glen Cove, NY

Let me start by saying that I LOVE my job (how could I not?), but if we're going total fantasy, I'd say a spy, even though I'm a terrible liar. I have no poker face whatsoever. What I really like is to travel, so maybe a food writer that goes all over the world exploring, collecting beautiful things, and in search of that perfect bite. Or I'd like to be Bear Grylls apprentice, but I'd probably want a bath and a real bed every now and then.

OLD FAVES

I love to put a new spin on a classic dish; you know, taking foods that we all loved as kids, dusting them off, and tweaking the flavors just enough so that we fall in love with those dishes all over again. At my restaurants, I like to use a classic dish, like a pierogi or ravioli, to introduce people to new cuts of meat or a new vegetable that they may not be familiar with or are afraid to try. By adding those ingredients to a dish people have known their whole lives, I find they are more willing to experiment with new things. I think what keeps people interested in food is that there are countless ways to make a dish. And even though the classics like meatballs, fried chicken, and mac and cheese rule the world, everyone gets a little tired of making the same recipes over and over again. So here we've taken some dishes that we all hold dear to our hearts and put a little spin on them just to keep things exciting.

—MICHAEL SYMON

NEW FLAVES

Bacon, Egg, and Cheese Boats

Serves: 8   **Prep Time:** 20 minutes   **Cook Time:** 25 minutes

I love a New York City, super-greasy, bacon, egg, and cheese on a roll from the deli down the street from my apartment. I really wanted to try to re-create that flavor for my next party, so I thought, why not try a bacon, egg, and cheese in a roll? **It's fantastic and so easy to make**, and the presentation elevates the classic deli-style sandwich into a meal perfect for your next brunch party.

½ pound thick-cut bacon, diced

4 demi-baguettes

8 large eggs

¼ cup heavy cream

1 cup Gruyère, shredded

¼ cup chives, chopped

Salt and freshly ground black pepper. to taste

FOR THE SALAD:

2 teaspoons Dijon mustard

1 lemon, juiced

¼ cup olive oil

Salt, to taste

Freshly ground black pepper

5-ounce box of mixed greens

½ a red onion, sliced

MARIO'S "DON'T WASTE IT" TIP

Don't throw away those scraps of bread that you've hollowed out of the baguettes. Turn them into bread crumbs. Just grind them up in the food processor, toast them in a 350°F oven until golden brown, and store in your pantry.

1. Preheat oven to 350°F.

2. In a sauté pan over medium-high heat, cook the bacon until crispy. Remove to a paper towel–lined plate and allow to cool.

3. Carefully make a V-shaped cut along the center of a each baguette, leaving about a half-inch left in the bottom. Scoop out the center of the bread. Place the baguettes on a baking sheet.

4. In a large mixing bowl, whisk together the eggs, heavy cream, bacon, Gruyère, and chives. Season with salt and freshly ground pepper. Pour the egg mixture into the baguette and place in the oven. Bake for 20 minutes, or until the eggs are puffed and slightly moist in the center. The eggs will continue to cook for a few minutes after they've been removed from the oven. When cool enough to handle, cut each baguette into 4 slices and serve alongside a salad.

FOR THE SALAD:

5. Whisk together Dijon mustard, the juice of a lemon, and olive oil, and season with salt and pepper. In a mixing bowl, toss mixed greens and red onion in with the dressing.

Blackberry–Brown Sugar Swirl Pancakes with Bacon-Bourbon Maple Syrup

Serves: 12   Prep Time: 7 minutes   Cook Time: 20 minutes

These pancakes are a family staple that I like to make on the weekends in the Batali house. I find that the key to making delicious pancakes is not only that you make sure not to overmix the batter but that you also let the batter rest for a little while and even overnight. What makes these pancakes extra special is the sweet blackberry swirl that perfectly complements the saltiness of the bacon.

FOR THE BLACKBERRY SAUCE:

2 cups blackberries

¼ cup granulated sugar

FOR THE BROWN SUGAR PANCAKES:

2 cups all-purpose flour

1 tablespoon baking powder

1 pinch of salt

1 tablespoon granulated sugar

2 eggs

1¾ cups whole milk

½ teaspoon vanilla extract

2 tablespoons butter, melted, plus more for the sauté pan

3 tablespoons light brown sugar

FOR THE BACON-BOURBON MAPLE SYRUP:

8 ounces thick-cut bacon, ½-inch pieces

¼ cup bourbon

2 cups maple syrup

Powdered sugar for serving

FOR THE BLACKBERRY SAUCE:

1. Combine blackberries and sugar in a small saucepan over medium-high heat. Bring to a simmer and cook, stirring frequently, until blackberries break down and a sauce forms, about 10 minutes. Set aside in bowl and let cool. Blend in a food processor or blender until smooth. Pour sauce into a pastry bag fitted with a medium-size tip.

FOR THE BROWN SUGAR PANCAKES:

2. Preheat a large nonstick sauté pan or griddle over medium heat.

3. In a medium bowl, whisk the flour, baking powder, salt, and granulated sugar together. In a large bowl, beat the eggs with the milk. Add the vanilla extract and the melted butter. Whisk to combine.

4. Add the dry ingredients into the wet ingredients in 3 batches. Make sure to get all the lumps out of the batter. Melt remaining butter in preheated pan. When foam subsides, pour a 2–3 ounce ladleful of batter into the pan (per pancake). Sprinkle some brown sugar over the top of the pancake. Then drizzle the jam in a swirled pattern starting from the center of the pancake and working your way to the edges. Cook the pancake until bubbles begin to form and the bottom is golden brown; then flip. Cook the pancake on the opposite side until golden brown and cooked through. Repeat with the remaining pancake batter and blackberry sauce. Set the pancakes aside.

FOR THE BACON-BOURBON MAPLE SYRUP:

5. Meanwhile, preheat a medium sauté pan over medium-high heat. Add bacon and sauté until crisp. Remove the bacon from the pan with a slotted spoon and set aside. Add bourbon and maple syrup to a separate sauté pan and place over high heat. Let the alcohol from the

bourbon cook off, about 2 minutes. Add the reserved bacon back into the sauce and remove from heat.

6. Serve the blackberry–brown sugar swirl pancakes with warm bacon-bourbon syrup. Dust with powdered sugar if desired.

MICHAEL'S "PANCAKE" TIP

Hey guys, if you're making pancakes for a crowd, just keep the oven on low to keep the pancakes warm on a sheet pan, and cover with foil until the party starts.

Hash Brown Frittata

Serves: 6   **Prep Time:** 5 minutes   **Cook Time:** 10–15 minutes

This dish combines two things I love for brunch: crispy potatoes and fluffy eggs. It's truly a match made in heaven. This dish honestly **comes together in no time** because I use store-bought frozen hash browns; they are my new favorite shortcut. They are just potatoes that have been blanched and rinsed, and I love to keep them in my freezer because they really cut the amount of work I have to do in the morning. I find that they also get crispier than any potato that I could make myself. All around, this dish is a winner and such a cool new way to have eggs and potatoes.

3 tablespoons canola oil

6 cups shredded frozen hash browns, thawed and drained

1 medium leek, whites and green parts only, root ends trimmed, cut in half lengthwise, and sliced

1 cup sliced cremini mushrooms

1 cup broccoli, cut into small florets

1 tablespoon olive oil

1 tablespoon butter

5 eggs

¼ cup whole milk

⅓ cup Parmesan, plus more for garnish

Salt and freshly ground black pepper, to taste

Parsley for garnish

1. Preheat oven to broil.

2. In a medium nonstick skillet, heat the canola oil. Add the hash browns to the pan and season with salt and pepper. Allow the hash browns to cook without moving, so they can begin to brown. Flip when bottom is golden and continue cooking the second side until golden. Remove from the pan and set aside.

3. Add the olive oil and butter to the nonstick pan over medium-high heat. When the butter has melted, add the leeks and cook until they begin to soften, about 2–3 minutes. Add the mushrooms and cook for a few minutes more, allowing the mushrooms to brown. Stir in the broccoli florets and cook for 2 more minutes.

4. While the vegetables are cooking, whisk together the eggs, milk, and Parmesan in a large mixing bowl. Season with salt and pepper. Pour egg mixture over the vegetables and stir, allowing the egg mixture to slightly scramble. Once it is almost set, remove from the heat and place the hash browns on top. Broil on high for 2-3 minutes until crispy and golden. Remove from oven, slice into wedges, and serve immediately.

Grilled Cheese Español

Serves: 1   **Prep Time:** 5 minutes   **Cook Time:** 30 minutes

I went to high school in Madrid, and although I missed the classic American dishes that I was used to eating in the states, I found so many new and interesting flavors in Spain that I could really play around with. When I would come home from school, I loved to make myself an after-school snack, and as I experienced more and more of the Spanish culture, those ingredients made their way into my cooking. **This sandwich is a classic** example of that: serrano ham and manchego cheese really took what I knew as a grilled cheese sandwich to the next level.

1 tablespoon extra-virgin olive oil

1 tablespoon butter

½ a yellow onion, sliced

Pinch of saffron

2 slices crusty Italian bread, ½-inch slices

2 tablespoons Dijon mustard

¼ cup grated manchego cheese

3–4 slices thinly sliced serrano ham

2–3 piquillo peppers, cut to lay flat

Salt and freshly ground black pepper, to taste

1. Heat the olive oil and butter in a large sauté pan over medium heat. Add the onions, season with salt, and cook for 10 minutes, stirring frequently. Add a splash of water to deglaze the pan. Reduce the heat to low and continue to cook for an additional 20 minutes, stirring occasionally, until the onions are well caramelized. Stir in the saffron and set aside.

TO ASSEMBLE THE GRILLED CHEESE:

2. Butter one side of 2 pieces of bread. Place 2 slices of bread, butter-side down, on a clean work surface. Spread the other sides of the bread slices with Dijon mustard. Place a good amount of caramelized onions on top of the bread. Then top with serrano ham, piquillo peppers, and shredded manchego cheese. Finish with the final piece of bread, butter-side out.

3. Preheat a nonstick pan over medium heat. Cooking in batches, add the sandwiches and cook until golden brown. Weigh the sandwich down with a brick or a cast-iron grill press. Flip and cook the other side until golden brown.

Fried Chicken Reuben

Serves: 5   **Prep Time:** *20 minutes*   **Cook Time:** *20 minutes*

I love fried chicken and coleslaw, and I love corned beef and cabbage. Well, do you know what you get when you combine those two magical dishes together? A fried chicken Reuben! That's right, and it's crazy good: crispy chicken, creamy coleslaw, gooey Jack cheese, and spicy honey mustard. Top that with some rye bread and you've got **one heck of a party going on in your mouth.**

5 chicken breasts, boneless, skinless, about 6 ounces each

2 cups all-purpose flour, for dredging

3 eggs, whisked

3 cups panko bread crumbs

1–2 teaspoons cayenne pepper

1 tablespoon onion powder

1 tablespoon garlic powder

10 slices rye bread

2 cups Monterey Jack cheese, grated

Spicy honey mustard to serve

¼ cup vegetable oil

Salt and freshly ground black pepper, to taste

FOR THE COLESLAW:

¾ cup mayonnaise

3 tablespoons apple-cider vinegar

2 teaspoons celery seed

2 tablespoons each of sugar, salt, and pepper

2 tablespoons olive oil

½ head green cabbage, sliced thinly

½ head purple cabbage, sliced thinly

1 large carrot, finely shredded

1. Preheat the oven broiler. Cut each chicken breast in half and pound thin, to about ¼-inch to ½-inch thick.

2. Place the flour, eggs, and panko in separate dishes large enough for dredging. Season each with salt and pepper.

3. Add the cayenne pepper, onion, and garlic powder to the flour and stir to combine.

4. Dredge the chicken first in the flour, shaking off the excess. Then dip in the eggs and dredge in the panko, pressing on the bread crumbs so they stick.

5. Place a large nonstick sauté pan over medium-high heat and add about ¼ cup of vegetable oil.

6. Cook the chicken, working in batches, until golden brown, about 3–4 minutes per side. Remove to a resting rack set inside a sheet tray and season with salt. Place the slices of bread on a sheet tray and top with the Monterey Jack cheese. Place in the oven and bake until melted, about 4–5 minutes.

7. Remove from the oven and assemble sandwiches.

8. Place a piece of chicken on top of a cheesy slice of bread; then add a piece of chicken, smear the chicken with honey mustard, and finally top with some creamy slaw. Close the sandwich with another piece of cheesy bread.

9. Serve warm and enjoy!

FOR THE COLESLAW:

10. In a large mixing bowl, add the mayonnaise, vinegar, celery seed, and sugar. Whisk in the oil and combine. Add the cabbages and carrots and toss to combine. Season with salt and pepper, and taste to adjust seasoning.

Pork Chop Cheesesteak

Serves: 4   Prep Time: *10 minutes*   Cook Time: *10 minutes*

Typically, I reserve this dish for leftovers, but sometimes **I get such a craving for it**, I have to make it from scratch. Now the classic Philly-style cheesesteak is hard to beat, but I live in New York, and unless I'm planning a road trip, it's not going to happen. So I turn to the next best thing. My pork cheesesteak is fantastic: it has all of the flavors that are so important in this sandwich and a couple of new ingredients that really make it sing.

3 boneless pork chops

3 tablespoons olive oil

Salt and freshly ground black pepper, to taste

2 red bell peppers, sliced

2 serrano peppers, sliced

1 onion, sliced

4 ounces sliced provolone

Sambal Oelek, to taste

4 hoagie rolls, split and toasted

1. Preheat a griddle over medium-high heat and drizzle with olive oil. Slice the pork chops into ½-inch slices, season with salt and pepper, and place on the griddle. Cook for 3–4 minutes without moving the pork chops so that they get nice and caramelized. Flip the pieces.

2. Scatter the bell peppers, serranos, and onions on the griddle. Season with salt. Griddle until peppers and onions have caramelized, about 5 minutes.

3. Add the pork to the griddle and cook until hot and crispy, about 5 minutes. Top with cheese and cook until the cheese has melted. Divide among the buns and top with the peppers. Spread sambal on the inside of the roll, to taste. Press sandwiches then slice and serve.

Mario and his son Leo

Whipped Piña Colada Dip

Serves: 4   **Prep Time:** 1 minute

This is a perfect treat to satisfy your sweet tooth, and what is **totally mind-blowing** about this is that it comes together in under a minute! Here I took all of the flavors that make up a classic piña colada, minus the rum, and pureed them all together to make a delicious frozen dip that is perfect for any poolside party.

1 cup frozen pineapple chunks

1 banana, cut into chunks and frozen

¼ cup coconut milk

Graham crackers, for serving

Pretzels sticks, for serving

Strawberries, for serving

1. Combine the frozen pineapple, banana, and coconut milk in the carafe of a blender. Blend until mixture is smooth and fluffy.

2. Serve immediately with graham crackers, pretzels, and whole strawberries for dipping. You can also keep this in the freezer and let sit for about five minutes before serving.

CLINTON'S "REPELLENT" TIP
Next time you're entertaining outside and you want to keep those pesky bugs away, try my bug-repelling centerpiece. Just add water, a few basil leaves, some lemon slices, and four or five drops of citronella oil to a mason jar, and float a tea candle on top. You'll send those bugs packing in no time.

Cheesy Pull-Apart Pesto Bread

Serves: 12   Prep Time: 5 minutes   Cook Time: 20 minutes

Every single time I make this dish, **people go crazy for it**; and it's so simple that you don't even have to make anything from scratch . . . it's the ultimate cheat! And if you're going to throw a party, sometimes you need a little help from the grocery store—you know? It's got everything you want in a garlic bread and more. First I drizzle this baby with butter, then I stuff it with cheese and slather it with tangy pesto. It's like garlic knots gone wild!

1 loaf French or Italian bread

¼ cup melted butter

1 cup store-bought basil pesto

1½ cups 3-cheese blend
(mozzarella, Parmesan, and
Asiago)

1. Preheat oven to 375°F.

2. Place the bread on a cutting board. Use a serrated knife to make 1-inch diagonal cuts through the bread, leaving the bottom crust intact. Turn the bread and make diagonal cuts in the opposite direction, creating a crosshatch pattern.

3. Meanwhile, pour the melted butter into the slits of the bread. Then use a spoon to drip the pesto into the cuts of the bread. Finally, stuff the shredded cheese into the cuts of the bread.

4. Wrap the bread in aluminum foil and place on a baking sheet. Place in the oven to bake for 15 minutes. Then open the foil to expose the top of the bread and cook for an additional 10 minutes.

5. Remove from the oven and let cool slightly before serving.

Crab Cake Phyllo Cups with Spicy Rémoulade

Serves: 30   Prep Time: 10 minutes   Cook Time: 10–12 minutes

These spicy little crab cups are such **a great dish to serve around the holidays.** I was inspired by a classic crab cake, which although delicious can be are very time-consuming. (If you're cooking for a crowd, you'll be in the kitchen for hours, and no one wants that). They are also a little lighter than the classic crab cake because there's not a ton of breading and they are baked not fried.

30 mini-phyllo shells, store-bought

1 pound lump crab meat, picked through for shell

2 tablespoons mayonnaise

2 teaspoons seafood seasoning

2 tablespoons chives, finely chopped

FOR THE SPICY RÉMOULADE SAUCE:

1 cup mayonnaise

3 tablespoons whole grain mustard

1 tablespoon Louisiana-style hot sauce

2 teaspoons seafood seasoning

2 tablespoons ketchup

2 tablespoons chives

2 tablespoons parsley

Juice of ½ lemon

2 tablespoons capers, drained and chopped

Salt and freshly ground black pepper, to taste

1. Preheat oven to 350°F. Spray 2 mini-cupcake tins with nonstick cooking spray.

2. Fill the tins with mini-phyllo cups. Set aside.

3. In a large bowl, fold the lump crab meat, mayonnaise, seafood seasoning, and chives until just combined. Fill each phyllo cup with the crab mixture. Place in the oven to bake for 10–12 minutes.

4. Remove from the oven and serve warm or at room temperature, topped with a small dollop of spicy rémoulade sauce.

FOR THE SPICY RÉMOULADE SAUCE:

5. Combine all the ingredients for the rémoulade sauce in a medium bowl. Season with salt and pepper to taste. Serve on top of phyllo cups.

Clam Chowder Fritter

Serves: 20   **Prep Time: 15 minutes**   **Cook Time: 10 minutes**

I made this dish last year for Super Bowl Sunday in honor of the New England Patriots. I wanted to take all of the flavors of a classic New England clam chowder and turn it into something that you could **eat with your hands.** So I decided to make fritters. These little gems have all of the delicious flavors of the classic soup in a perfectly fried package that's ideal for any game-day feast. Go, team!

3 medium Yukon gold potatoes, peeled and diced into ¼-inch cube

1 cup water

½ cup butter

1 cup flour

¼ teaspoon salt

4 large eggs

½ pound clams, chopped

2 strips thick-cut bacon, cooked and diced

2 tablespoons chopped chives, plus more to garnish

Vegetable oil, for frying

FOR THE CHOWDER SAUCE:

1 bay leaf

1 cup milk

2 tablespoons flour

2 tablespoons butter

1 teaspoon fresh thyme, chopped

3 tablespoons clam juice

Salt and freshly ground black pepper, to taste

1. Place diced potatoes in a medium saucepan and cover with cold water. Place on medium-high heat and let come to a boil. Cook until the potatoes are tender (but do not fall apart), about 15 minutes. Drain and set aside to cool.

2. Fill a Dutch oven ⅔ way with oil and heat to 350°F.

3. While the oil is heating, combine water and butter in a medium saucepan and bring to boil. Remove the pan from the heat and add in the flour and salt, stirring with a wooden spoon until the dough pulls away from the sides. Add the eggs to the batter one at a time, fully incorporating each before adding the next.

4. When the batter has come together, remove from the heat and fold in the cooked potatoes, chopped clams, bacon, and chives.

5. Using a small ice cream scoop, drop the batter into the oil and fry until golden brown, about 2–3 minutes. Remove to a paper towel–lined plate and season with salt.

6. Garnish with more chives and serve with chowder dipping sauce.

FOR THE CHOWDER SAUCE:

7. Add the milk and bay leaf to a small saucepan and heat to a simmer. Lower the heat and remove the bay leaf.

8. In a medium saucepan, make a roux by melting the butter and whisking in the flour to combine. Let roux cook for 2–3 minutes, stirring occasionally, until golden but not burnt. Slowly add in the warm milk, whisking continuously until the mixture begins to thicken. Whisk in the clam juice and thyme, and season with salt and pepper.

9. Serve with the fritters.

Sweet Potato Gnocchi with Brussels Sprouts and Brown Butter

Serves: 8   **Prep Time:** 30 minutes   **Cook Time:** 1 hour, 25 minutes

This is **one of my go-to dishes** when the weather gets a little cold and the leaves start to change, and I begin to get excited about the fall. It happens around the same time that sweet potatoes and Brussels sprouts are in the market, and I want something satisfying and hearty that reminds me a little of the Thanksgiving feast that is only weeks away (but with flavors that are truly seasonal).

FOR THE SWEET POTATO GNOCCHI:

2 pounds sweet potatoes, washed and pierced (about 3 potatoes)

12 ounces whole milk ricotta, strained for 4 hours or overnight

1½ teaspoons nutmeg, freshly grated

1 large egg

1 cup Parmesan, freshly grated

1 teaspoon salt

1½ cups almond flour

2½ cups all-purpose flour, plus more for dusting

FOR THE SAUCE:

4 cups Brussels sprouts, ends trimmed and thinly sliced

4 tablespoons unsalted butter

½ cup sage leaves

¼ cup parsley, chopped

Parmesan, freshly grated

Olive oil

Salt and freshly ground black pepper, to taste

FOR THE SWEET POTATO GNOCCHI:

1. Preheat oven to 400°F.

2. Place 1 cup of kosher salt in a mound on a sheet tray, then gently shake it out to form a base for your sweet potatoes. Place the potatoes on the salt and bake for 60–75 minutes (until tender when pierced with a paring knife). Remove from the oven, slice in half lengthwise, and let them cool.

3. Meanwhile, in a large mixing bowl, combine the strained ricotta, nutmeg, egg, and Parmesan. Scoop the potato flesh out of the skin and push through a ricer over the ricotta mixture. Discard the skins. Season with 1 teaspoon salt, then begin to incorporate both flours, being sure not to work the dough too much. Gently bring together to form one dough mass, then place on a lightly floured surface.

4. Line a few sheet trays with parchment paper, then dust the parchment with flour. Begin cutting off pieces of dough and rolling into logs about ½-inch wide. Do this on a lightly floured surface with your fingers spread apart. With a sharp paring knife, cut ¾-inch-wide pieces from the log, forming your gnocchi. Give them another dusting of flour before transferring to your prepared sheet tray in an even layer. Place in the fridge or freezer while you repeat with the remaining dough.

FOR THE SAUCE:

5. Bring a large pot of salted water to a boil.

6. Place a large sauté pan over medium-high heat. When the pan is hot, add the butter and sage. Cook until the butter begins to brown. Then add the Brussels sprouts and sauté until caramelized.

7. Meanwhile, drop your gnocchi and cook for 1–2 minutes, until they float. Add the gnocchi to the pan with the Brussels sprouts. Add a few tablespoons of pasta water and cook for an additional minute. Remove from heat and sprinkle with Parmesan and chopped parsley.

Chicken Thigh Osso Buco with Creamy Polenta

| Serves: 4 | Prep Time: 15 minutes | Cook Time: 55 minutes |

This is a really easy at-home version of a classic Italian dish called osso buco. Now osso buco is a braised dish traditionally made with veal and served over polenta; it can take hours to make, but with my chicken-thigh version, **you'll have dinner on the table in no time.**

8 chicken thighs, bone-in, skin on

½ cup all-purpose flour

Salt and freshly ground black pepper, to taste

1 onion, diced

1 carrot, peeled, diced

1 stalk celery, diced

2 cloves garlic, minced

1 tablespoon tomato paste

1 cup white wine

2 cups chicken stock

1 sprig rosemary

3 sprigs thyme

FOR THE POLENTA:

1 cup yellow cornmeal

1 teaspoon salt

3 tablespoons butter

2 tablespoons Parmesan, grated

FOR THE CLASSIC GREMOLATA:

¼ cup parsley, finely chopped

1 clove garlic, minced

1 lemon, zested

Salt and pepper

1. Place the flour on a shallow plate and season with salt and pepper. Dredge the chicken thighs in the seasoned flour, shaking off the excess.

2. In a large Dutch oven over medium heat, add olive oil. Sear the chicken thighs until browned on both sides, browning in batches if necessary. Remove browned thighs to a plate.

3. Add the onion, carrot, and celery, and sauté until soft and translucent, about 5 minutes. Add 2 cloves minced garlic and cook until fragrant, about 1 more minute. Add tomato paste and allow to brown another minute or so. Add the meat back to the pan, then add the wine, and reduce by half. Tie the herbs together with a piece of kitchen twine and add to the pot. Pour in the chicken stock and bring to a boil. Reduce heat to low, cover and simmer 45 minutes until chicken is cooked through. Remove tied herbs and discard.

4. In the meantime, make the polenta: in a large saucepan, bring 5 cups of water to a boil. Whisking, gradually add the cornmeal in a steady stream. Add salt and turn down the heat to medium and cook until thickened, whisking frequently, about 10 minutes. Remove from the heat and stir in butter and cheese.

FOR THE CLASSIC GREMOLATA:

5. Chop together parsley, remaining garlic clove and lemon zest. Drizzle with a bit of olive oil, and season with salt and pepper.

TO SERVE:

6. Spoon a bit of polenta on the plate, then top with 2 chicken thighs, a spoonful of the cooking liquid, and vegetables. Top with gremolata.

Chicken Meatballs Marsala

Serves: 4   **Prep Time:** 10 minutes   **Cook Time:** 20 minutes

This is **one of my most popular recipes** on the TheChew.com and I made it on the fly during a pantry raid challenge that Clinton Kelly forced me to do. I had to gather a bunch of pantry ingredients to go with a mystery protein that turned out to be ground chicken. Turns out, I'm kind of good at this cooking thing. And really, how can you go wrong with meatballs and marsala?

3 tablespoons olive oil

1 pound ground chicken

1 cup ricotta cheese, drained

1 egg, beaten

2 cloves garlic, finely grated

¼ cup flat-leaf parsley, roughly chopped

⅔ cup panko bread crumbs

A few gratings of nutmeg

½ cup freshly grated Parmesan

1 tablespoon flour

Salt and freshly ground black pepper, to taste

Olive oil

1 pound mushrooms, cremini or white, thinly sliced

3 shallots, separated

1 cup marsala wine

3 tablespoons butter, cubed

1. In a large sauté pan over high heat, add 2 tablespoons olive oil until shimmering.

2. In a large bowl, add chicken, ricotta, egg, garlic, 1 finely grated shallot, ¼-cup parsley, panko bread crumbs, nutmeg, and Parmesan. Sprinkle with flour. Season with salt and pepper. Form mixture into balls and fry until golden brown. Remove and set aside.

3. Heat remaining olive oil in sauté pan over high heat, then add mushrooms and 2 sliced shallots. Season with salt and pepper. Cook over high heat, letting the mushrooms brown.

4. Add the marsala wine. Reduce for 1 minute. Stir in butter, swirling to emulsify. Return the meatballs back to the pan, toss until well coated.

CLINTON'S "FULL DISCLOSURE" TIP
When I'm throwing a party, whether it's potluck or just buffet style, I always make little ID cards for each dish. That way I'm not spending the entire party answering questions about whether a dish is vegetarian or gluten free! It's all written right there on the card.

Grilled Cheese and Tomato Casserole

Serves: *8*   **Prep Time:** *20 minutes*   **Cook Time:** *40 minutes*

This crazy casserole **combines two of my favorite things** in the whole entire world: grilled cheese and tomato soup! When I've been out in the cold weather, especially when it's snowing, I just crave this soul-soothing combo. It's truly the best of both worlds.

1 crusty sourdough peasant loaf, cut into ½-inch slices

1 pound deli-sliced aged cheddar cheese

1 cup fresh basil leaves, plus more to garnish

1 stick unsalted butter, softened

3 tablespoons extra-virgin olive oil

1 medium onion, grated

3 garlic cloves, grated

4½ ounces tomato paste

1 tablespoon paprika

2 teaspoons fresh thyme leaves

1 teaspoon red pepper flakes

1 cup milk

½ cup heavy cream

6 eggs

¼ cup Monterey Jack Cheese, grated

¼ cup aged cheddar cheese, grated

1. Preheat oven to 325°F. Lightly grease a 9x9-inch baking dish with cooking spray.

2. Butter both sides of each piece of bread and season with salt and pepper. Place on a baking sheet and cook until golden, flipping once, about 8 minutes. Build sandwiches using 2 slices of bread, 3 slices of cheese, and 2 or 3 basil leaves. The basil should be placed between the slices of cheese. Cut the sandwiches into 4 pieces each.

3. Heat a large sauté pan over medium-high heat with olive oil. Add the onions and sauté until lightly caramelized, seasoning with salt, about 3 minutes. Add the garlic, tomato paste, paprika, thyme, and pepper flakes, and cook until paste is fragrant and rust-like in color.

4. Reduce heat to low and whisk in milk and cream. Season with salt and pepper and bring to a boil.

5. Remove from heat and ladle a small amount of the warm sauce into a bowl with the eggs and whisk to temper. Pour in the remaining sauce from the pan and whisk to combine.

6. Shingle the sandwiches into the prepared baking dish and pour the egg mixture over. Sprinkle on the grated cheeses and bake for 30 minutes until golden brown on top.

7. Serve warm with a garnish of sliced basil.

Beer-Can Turkey

Serves: 12　　**Prep Time: 5 minutes**　　**Cook Time: 2 hours, 30 minutes**

Everybody loves beer can chicken because the whole chicken gets crispy and brown when you cook it on the grill, and the inside stays moist and juicy from the beer. So I began to wonder . . . could I do this with a turkey for Thanksgiving? It turns out the answer is yes, and it only takes 2½ hours to cook! I'm telling you, you will never make turkey any other way ever again.

1 12-pound turkey, rinsed and patted dry, cavity cleaned

2 25¼-ounce cans of lager-style beer

1 cup water

FOR THE DRY RUB:

3 tablespoons dried oregano

3 tablespoons garlic powder

2 tablespoons smoked paprika

2 tablespoons coriander, toasted and ground

1 tablespoon freshly ground black pepper

2 teaspoons kosher salt

Juice of 1 lemon

1. Preheat grill to 350°F.

2. Using a can opener, remove the top from one of the beers. Pour a third of the beer into the roasting pan, then set the open can of beer in the center.

3. Combine the oregano, garlic powder, smoked paprika, coriander, salt, and pepper in a small bowl. Place the turkey on a cutting board. Squeeze lemon juice all over the inside and outside of the turkey. Rub the spice mix all over the outside and inside the cavity of the bird. Put extra seasoning inside the opened beer can. Place the seasoned turkey on top of the beer can, with the legs down. Pour half of the second beer into the bottom of the roasting pan along with 1 cup of water. Carefully place on the grill, being very careful to stabilize the bird. Close the lid of the grill and cook for 1 hour. Open the grill and pour the other half of the beer over the turkey. Close the grill and cook for 1 more hour. Then baste the turkey with juices from the bottom of the pan. If the turkey begins to look a little dark, tent the top with foil. Let cook for another 30 minutes, or until the internal temperature of the leg reaches 165°F.

4. Remove from the grill and baste one more time before tenting with foil and resting for 30 minutes. After 30 minutes, slice and serve!

Brioche-Encrusted Ham

Serves: 12   **Prep Time:** 15 minutes   **Cook Time:** 2 hours

Ham is so popular around the holidays that I thought it might be fun to play around with some new and interesting ways to roast it. Why not wrap it in bread dough so that you've got the ham and the sandwich in one dish? **This dish is so impressive** that I like to carve it table-side. It's also perfect for leftovers, which in my family begin anytime after the meal from midnight throughout the following day.

1 7–10 pound smoked boneless ham

2 pounds store-bought brioche dough

1 cup red pepper jelly

1 egg plus 1 tablespoon water, whisked, for egg wash

1. Score the ham by making shallow cuts in a crosshatch pattern. Allow the ham to come to room temperature.

2. Preheat oven to 425°F.

3. Roll out the brioche dough to ¼-inch thick in the shape of an oval. Spread the red pepper jelly evenly over the dough, leaving a 1-inch border. Place the ham in the middle of the dough and spread more of the jelly on top of the ham. Bring the sides of the dough up to cover the ham completely, pinching the corners together and twisting into a knot. Using the egg wash, brush the edges to seal the dough shut.

4. Carefully lift the ham onto a baking sheet lined with parchment paper. Brush with the egg wash and place the ham in the oven. Immediately reduce the temperature to 350°F and let the ham cook for 2 hours, or until the internal temperature is 160°F. You may need to tent the ham halfway through to prevent the crust from becoming too dark.

5. Remove the ham from the oven and allow to cool for at least 15 minutes. Slice the ham and serve.

FOR LEFTOVERS:

Serve any remaining ham on mini-brioche rolls with Chianti mustard and salsa verde.

Greek Lamb Wellington

Serves: 6   **Prep Time: 5 minutes**   **Cook Time: 15 minutes**

I used to make this dish at my restaurant, Lola, and it was a big hit with my customers. It's reminiscent of a classic Wellington, which is typically made with beef and then wrapped with puff pastry. But **the flavors are completely different.** For my Greek Wellington, I take an entire lamb loin and drape it in tangy grape leaves and then wrap it in phyllo dough. It has all of the flavors that make up a good Greek dinner, but it's prepared in a decidedly English manner.

2 pounds boneless lamb loin

Salt and freshly ground black pepper, to taste

2 tablespoons rosemary, finely chopped

16-ounce jar of grape leaves (about 8 leaves), stems removed

4-6 tablespoons melted unsalted butter

4 sheets phyllo dough

Lemon juice

Olive oil

1. Preheat oven to 425°F.

2. Season the lamb with salt, pepper, and rosemary, coating it on all sides. Drape the grape leaves over the loin, overlapping them and covering it completely. Allow the lamb to come to room temperature for 30 minutes before baking.

3. Lay out the first sheet of phyllo and brush the entire surface with butter. Place the second sheet on top, then continue the process until you have 4 sheets layered. Brush the final sheet with butter, then place the lamb, presentation-side down, in the center. Trim the sides on the right and left of the lamb loin with kitchen shears, leaving 1 inch on either side.

4. To fold, bring the bottom of the phyllo over the lamb, fold in the sides, then continue to roll up like a burrito. Brush the exposed phyllo dough each time you roll up the loin. Place on a parchment paper–lined sheet tray, seam-side down.

5. Brush the top and sides with the remaining melted butter. Place in the oven to bake for 15 minutes for medium rare. Remove from the oven and rest for 10 minutes.

6. Slice with a serrated knife into 1-inch pieces. Serve with a squeeze of lemon juice and a drizzle of olive oil.

The Chew: An Essential Guide to Cooking and Entertaining

Buche de Noel Cupcakes

Serves: 12   **Prep Time:** 5 minutes   **Cook Time:** 30 minutes

If there is one holiday dessert that **makes me jump for joy**, it's a Buche de Noel. It is so delicious with that creamy filling and chocolate coating. But it's so hard to make, so I've developed this cupcake version that's a cinch. It is great for a crowd, travels well, and I think is as good, if not better, than the real thing. But I'll let you be the judge.

FOR THE CUPCAKES:

4 tablespoons butter

¼ cup semisweet chocolate, melted

2 teaspoons vanilla extract

7 large eggs, separated

1½ cups granulated sugar, divided

½ teaspoon cream of tartar

1 cup flour

2¼ teaspoons baking powder

½ teaspoons salt

Powdered sugar, to decorate

FOR THE WHIPPED FILLING:

1 cup mascarpone cheese

1¼ cups powdered sugar

1 teaspoon amaretto liquor

Pinch of salt

FOR THE GLAZE:

1 cup bittersweet chocolate

½ cup semisweet chocolate

8 tablespoons butter

½ cup heavy cream

FOR THE CUPCAKES:

1. Preheat oven to 375°F. Butter a 12-count muffin tin and dust with flour.

2. Place chocolate and butter in a microwave-safe bowl and heat in 20-second intervals, stirring between intervals, until smooth. Stir in vanilla and set aside.

3. In a medium bowl, whip egg yolks and ½ cup of sugar until pale and tripled in volume, about 10 minutes. The yolks should hold a ribbon-like line when lifted. Stir in the chocolate mixture.

4. In a large bowl, whip egg whites until frothy. Continue to whip while slowly adding remaining sugar. Sprinkle in the cream of tartar and whip into soft peaks.

5. Whisk together the flour, baking powder, and salt in a bowl.

6. Alternate folding the egg whites and flour mixtures into the yolks until some streaks remain. Use a large ice cream scoop to transfer batter evenly to the prepared muffin tin. Bake for 12–14 minutes or until cupcakes spring back when touched.

7. Remove from oven and allow to cool completely in muffin tin.

8. Fill a small pastry bag fitted with a small tip with whipped filling. Place a hole in the top of each muffin and fill with about 2 tablespoons of filling. Using a spatula or butter knife, spread a small amount of glaze on top to cover. Use tool to make a wood-like pattern in glaze.

9. Place cupcakes in fridge to chill for 15 minutes. Dust heavily with powdered sugar to decorate.

FOR THE WHIPPED FILLING:

10. Whip the ingredients together until fully combined.

FOR THE GLAZE:

11. Place the chocolates and butter in a microwave-safe bowl and heat in 20-second intervals, stirring between intervals, until smooth. Remove and stir in cream until incorporated. Reheat in microwave for 10–20 seconds when ready to use.

Cheesecake with Pretzel Crust

Serves: 24   **Prep Time: 30 minutes**   **Cook Time: 1–1½ hours**

My grandfather Pap makes this every year for Thanksgiving, and I'm telling you people are skipping seconds on the turkey to save room for this dessert. With the pretzel crust and the strawberry jam that you pour over the top, **it's the perfect balance** between salty and sweet. Pap, you're a genius!

FOR THE CRUST:

1½ cups pretzels, ground

½ cup graham cracker, ground

¼ cup granulated sugar

8 tablespoons unsalted butter, melted

Pinch of salt

FOR THE FILLING:

24 ounces cream cheese, at room temperature

1 cup sour cream

1 cup granulated sugar

5 large eggs

1 teaspoon vanilla

10 ounces strawberry preserves, to serve

1. Preheat your oven to 300°F.

2. In a mixing bowl, combine the pretzel, graham cracker crumbs, sugar, and melted butter. Add a pinch of salt and then press into the bottom of a 13x9-inch clear glass baking dish. Set aside while you make your filling.

3. In the bowl of a mixer fitted with a paddle attachment, cream the softened cream cheese on medium speed, scraping the sides and the beater occasionally. Next add the sour cream and continue to mix until combined. Then add the sugar. With the mixer on low, add the eggs one at a time, thoroughly mixing in after each addition. Add the vanilla. Pour the filling over the crust and bake for 1 hour or until the center is no longer jiggly.

4. Remove the cheesecake from the oven and let sit for a few minutes while you prepare the jam. In a small saucepan, melt the strawberry jam over low heat. When it is melted, strain into another bowl (if you prefer no seeds). Pour the melted jam over the top of the cheesecake and smooth out into an even layer. Let the cheesecake sit out to cool for another 30 minutes to an hour, then slice into 24 squares while still warm. Refrigerate for a few hours to chill completely.

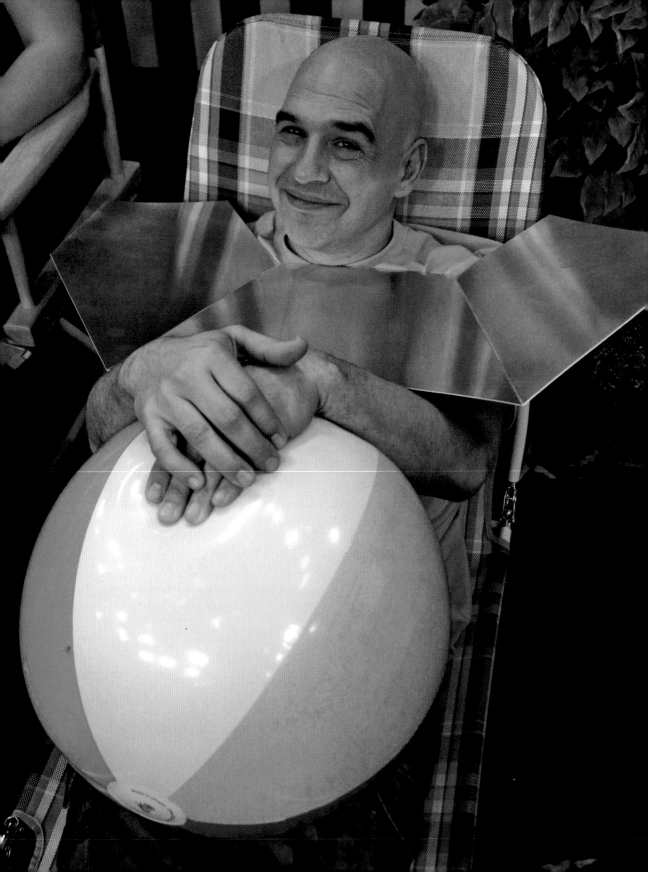

TURN YOUR CHARCOAL OR GAS GRILL INTO A SMOKER

Anyone who knows me knows I'm totally obsessed with BBQ. Tender brisket, baby back ribs, pulled pork sandwiches, and smoked sausages just call to me when summer comes around. I'm always on the lookout for ways to get restaurant-quality BBQ at home without having to spend that hard-earned cash on an expensive smoker. If you've got foil, wood chips, and a grill, well then you've got yourself a smoker. Whether your grill is charcoal or gas, just follow these easy steps and you'll be barbecuing like a pro in no time! —MICHAEL SYMON

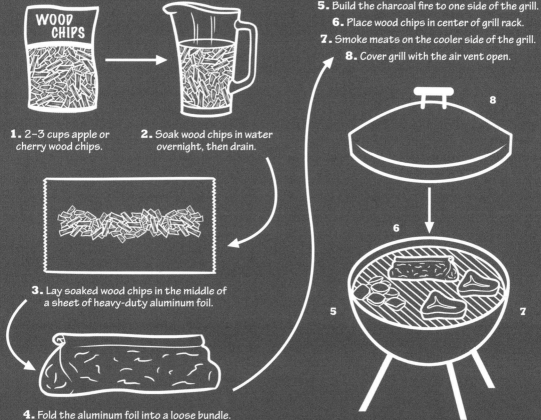

5. Build the charcoal fire to one side of the grill.
6. Place wood chips in center of grill rack.
7. Smoke meats on the cooler side of the grill.
8. Cover grill with the air vent open.

1. 2–3 cups apple or cherry wood chips.

2. Soak wood chips in water overnight, then drain.

3. Lay soaked wood chips in the middle of a sheet of heavy-duty aluminum foil.

4. Fold the aluminum foil into a loose bundle.

VIEWER Q&A
with MICHAEL SYMON

What is the first thing that you do when you arrive at the studio?
—Mae Purugganan, Albany, NY

I make myself a bowl of oatmeal and drink a green juice while I go over my scripts for the day. I also like to give Clinton a hard time in the hair and makeup room because I know how much he enjoys his quiet time in the mornings. It brings me great joy.

How did you meet and fall in love with Liz?
—Jacqueline Gawne, Chicago, IL

I met Liz while working in the restaurant business in 1989. She worked the front of the house and I cooked in the back. We were friends for a few years and then we started dating, fell in love, and, twenty-six years later, here we are still happily married.

If you could eat a meal with anyone, dead or alive, who would it be with?
—Lisa Clark, St. Michaels, MD

Absolutely, without a doubt, my grandfather, Pap. At ninety-seven years old, he is still always the life of the party. And if he's the one cooking the meal, then I'm in for a real treat! For me, there will never be anything better than a meal with my family.

What is the one dish that you never want to eat again?
—Stephanie Blumenthal, Rye Brook, NY

Oh, that's easy! Flourless chocolate cake with raspberry coulis. I hate raspberries; I'm sure you've heard me say it before, but I'll say it again: I hate them. I'm still bitter that they ruined chocolate desserts for an entire decade of my life.

GUILTY

When I think of a guilty pleasure, I think about something that isn't very good for me—but in the moment, I have to have it anyway. It could be cold pizza with raspberry jam by the light of the fridge at two o'clock in the morning, or a slice of pie that you sneak after lunch—but was actually meant for dinner—and then hide the evidence or chalk it up to recipe testing. When I was a kid it was cold, leftover spaghetti and meatballs that I would put between two slices of bread while I watched *The Tonight Show* or listened to Pink Floyd, depending on what kind of mood I was in. Regardless of the kind of meal, there is a sneakiness that I attach to a guilty pleasure that is almost more satisfying than the meal itself. So go ahead, be bad! **—MARIO BATALI**

PLEASURES

Ham, Egg, and Cheese Waffle Sandwich

Serves: 4   **Prep Time:** 5 minutes   **Cook Time:** 10 minutes

There is definitely a sense of urgency involved when putting together **a guilty pleasure dish.** It really can't take hours to make because when you get the urge for something bad, you need it right then and there. That's why this sandwich is so great. You can be devouring it in less than 10 minutes.

8 store-bought toaster waffles

4 slices store-bought pork roll

2 tablespoons butter

4 eggs

Salt and freshly ground black pepper, to taste

FOR THE FONDUE:

1 cup heavy cream

2 cups shredded Monterey Jack cheese

Pinch of grated nutmeg

Couple dashes of hot sauce

Salt and freshly ground black pepper, to taste

1. Heat a griddle pan over medium heat. Add the toaster waffles to the griddle and begin to toast, about a minute per side, until golden brown. Remove from griddle and set aside.

2. To each of the slices of pork roll, make three small slits equally spaced around the outer edge. This will prevent the ham from curling while cooking. Add about a tablespoon of butter to the griddle and spread it around one half while the butter melts. Place each of the ham slices on the buttered side of the grill and cook for about 2–3 minutes per side, until the ham has browned well.

3. Meanwhile, begin to heat the additional tablespoon of butter on the other half of the griddle. Crack the eggs onto the griddle leaving enough space between them. Season with salt and pepper and let cook for about a minute. Gently turn the eggs over, being sure not to crack the yolk. Cook for an additional 15 seconds for an over-easy egg.

4. To build the sandwiches, place a slice of the pork roll on one of the toaster waffles. Place an egg onto the ham slice. Drizzle fondue over the egg and place another toaster waffle on top. Build the other sandwiches by repeating with the remaining ingredients.

5. Serve immediately.

FOR THE FONDUE:

6. In a small saucepan over medium heat, begin to heat the heavy cream. When the cream starts to simmer, remove from heat and stir in the shredded cheese. Whisk continuously until thoroughly combined. Stir in the nutmeg and hot sauce. Season with salt and pepper. Keep warm until ready to use.

Cinna-Bacon Pie

Serves: 8   **Prep Time: 45 minutes**   **Cook Time: 1 hour**

Okay, this pie is **so over-the-top decadent**, it makes me blush just a little bit to describe it. It's basically an apple pie topped with cinnamon rolls sprinkled with bacon, and then drizzled with a sugar glaze. The salty-sweet flavor is so incredibly indulgent you'll want to sneak an extra slice later when no one's looking, and then maybe have it again for breakfast the next morning.

FOR THE CRUST:

1 teaspoon kosher salt

⅔ cup cold water

4 ounces thick-cut bacon, finely diced and frozen

4 cups all-purpose flour

1 cup unsalted butter, cut into ¼-inch-thick slices and chilled

FOR THE APPLE PIE FILLING:

2 teaspoons cornstarch

1 teaspoon vanilla extract

¼ cup, plus 1 tablespoon water

1 tablespoon unsalted butter

1 teaspoon canola oil

6 apples, a mix of tart and sweet, such as Granny Smith and Golden Delicious, cut into quarters, cored, and thinly sliced crosswise

⅓ cup packed light or dark brown sugar

1 teaspoon fresh lemon juice

½ teaspoon kosher salt

All-purpose flour, for rolling

FOR THE CINNAMON ROLL FILLING:

¼ cup melted butter

2 tablespoons cinnamon

¼ cup sugar

½ pound bacon, cooked

1. Preheat the oven to 350°F.

FOR THE CRUST:

2. In a small bowl, stir the salt into the cold water until it dissolves. In a separate bowl, use your hands to toss the bacon with flour until well coated. Pulse the flour and bacon in a food processor until coarse crumbs form. Return mixture to large bowl. Add the butter to the flour mixture and then press in the butter with your fingertips until coarse crumbs form with a few bigger pieces remaining. Add the salted water all at once, and quickly gather the dough with your hands into a large, shaggy clump. Divide the dough into 2 equal pieces, shape into disks, cover tightly with plastic wrap, and chill until firm, at least 30 minutes.

FOR THE APPLE PIE FILLING:

3. In a small bowl, stir together the cornstarch, vanilla, and ¼ cup of water until smooth. In a large skillet, melt the butter in the oil over medium-high heat. Add the apples and cook, stirring occasionally, until lightly charred, about 5 minutes. Add the brown sugar, lemon juice, and salt. Cook, stirring frequently, until the sugar dissolves, about 2 minutes. Add the cornstarch mixture and cook, stirring, until the liquid thickens, about 1 minute. Remove from the heat and let cool completely.

FOR THE CINNAMON ROLL FILLING:

4. Cook bacon until crispy, about 10–12 minutes. Chop into fine pieces and set aside.

5. On a lightly floured surface, and using a lightly floured rolling pin, roll one piece of dough into a ¼-inch-thick round. Transfer the round

FOR THE GLAZE:

2 cups powdered sugar

4 tablespoons melted butter

1 teaspoon vanilla

Pinch of salt

¼ cup milk, plus more if needed

of dough to a 9-inch round pie dish. Using your index finger and thumb, create fluted edges around the rim of the piecrust. Place the piecrust in the refrigerator to set for at least 15 minutes.

6. Meanwhile, roll out the second piecrust into a long oval shape, about 10 inches long and ¼-inch thick. Brush the melted butter onto the rolled-out dough. Next combine cinnamon and sugar in a small bowl and sprinkle on top of butter. Then sprinkle the crumbled bacon over the crust, reserving a few tablespoons for garnish if desired. Facing the crust horizontally, roll the crust in the style of a jelly roll. Cut into ½-inch-thick slices.

7. Pour the cooled apple filling into the prepared piecrust. Then place the cinnamon roll slices on top of the filling so that the pinwheel sides face up. Place in the oven and bake until golden brown, about 45 minutes. Cool completely on a wire rack.

FOR THE GLAZE:

8. Combine all ingredients in a large bowl. Drizzle over the top of the pie. Sprinkle reserved crumbled bacon on top if desired.

MICHAEL'S "BROWN SUGAR" TIP

Do you ever have that problem where you go to bake something with brown sugar and it's as hard as a rock? Well, here's a great tip for you, then: just place a piece of orange zest in the package or a little bit of apple peel, and you'll never have dried-out sugar again.

Mac and Cheese Florentine

This dish is great for brunch or a midnight snack if you're **craving something a little bit bad for you.** I'm always looking for new and interesting ways to use up leftovers, and I got really creative with this one. I was very pregnant when I came up with this, which is why it may have landed in the guilty pleasures section of the book.

2 cups of leftover Carla's Slow Cooker Mac and Cheese, chilled (page 81)

2 tablespoons butter

8 ounces baby spinach

¼ teaspoon freshly grated nutmeg

Salt and freshly ground black pepper, to taste

2 tablespoons distilled white vinegar

4 eggs

Hot sauce to taste

1. Pull your leftover Carla's Slow Cooker Mac and Cheese out of the refrigerator. Use a cookie cutter to cut out 4 round pieces.

2. Preheat a medium nonstick sauté pan over medium heat. Add 1 tablespoon of butter. When the butter has melted, add the spinach and sauté until just wilted. Season to taste with nutmeg, salt, and pepper. Remove spinach from pan, set aside, and keep warm.

3. Melt 1 tablespoon of butter in the sauté pan. Add the round pieces of mac and cheese and cook for 2–3 minutes. Flip the pieces to the other side and cook an additional 2–3 minutes, until golden brown and warmed through. Remove to a plate and set aside and covering to keep warm.

4. To poach the eggs, bring a medium pot of water to a simmer and add the vinegar. Drop each egg into the water and swirl the water to keep the eggs from sticking to the bottom. Cook the eggs for about 4 minutes, or until set, making sure that the water stays at a constant simmer during the cooking process.

5. Remove the eggs with a slotted spoon and drain on a towel.

6. Plate the cooked mac and cheese rounds with some spinach on top of each piece. Top each with a poached egg. Serve with hot sauce to taste.

MARIO'S "EGG" TIP
Did you know that you can poach an egg in the oven? You sure can; just set the oven to 250°F and place an oven-safe cereal bowl inside to heat. Pour hot water into the bowl and then crack the egg into the water. Let the egg sit, undisturbed, for about 6–7 minutes or until set. Drain and serve. I like to use this technique when I am poaching eggs for a crowd.

Spicy Queso Dip

Serves: 8   **Prep Time:** 10 minutes   **Cook Time:** 10 minutes

I don't know about you, but I'm a sucker for this stuff. When I go to a Tex-Mex restaurant and I see it on the menu, I have to order it. There is just something so magical about the combination of crunchy, salty chips and this spicy, cheesy dip. I would literally **lick the bowl clean** if no one was watching.

1 tablespoon olive oil

1 small white onion, very finely diced

1 red bell pepper, finely minced

2–3 jalapeños, minced

1 cup heavy cream

1 pound yellow American cheese, shredded

8 ounces pepper jack cheese, shredded

1 bunch cilantro leaves, chopped

Salt and freshly ground black pepper, to taste

Tortilla chips, to serve

1. Heat the olive oil in a pot over medium heat. Add the onion, bell pepper, jalapeño, and a generous pinch of salt, cooking until soft and translucent, about 8 minutes. Add the cream and bring to a simmer.

2. Add the cheese, stirring continuously, until it has all melted, and season to taste with salt and pepper.

3. Garnish with cilantro and serve with tortilla chips.

4. If entertaining, serve in an oven-safe bowl or crock that has been warmed in the oven.

Popcorn Shrimp

Serves: 6   Prep Time: 10 minutes   Cook Time: 10 minutes

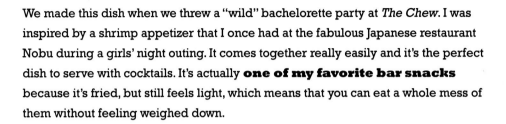

We made this dish when we threw a "wild" bachelorette party at *The Chew*. I was inspired by a shrimp appetizer that I once had at the fabulous Japanese restaurant Nobu during a girls' night outing. It comes together really easily and it's the perfect dish to serve with cocktails. It's actually **one of my favorite bar snacks** because it's fried, but still feels light, which means that you can eat a whole mess of them without feeling weighed down.

1 pound rock shrimp

2 cups rice flour, plus ½ cup to dredge

Salt, to taste

2 egg yolks

2 cups ice-cold seltzer

Vegetable oil, for frying

FOR THE DRESSING:

½ cup mayonnaise

2 tablespoons adobo sauce

2 tablespoons honey

Juice of ½ a lime

¼ cup chives, thinly sliced

1. Fill a Dutch oven ⅔ of the way up with oil. Heat to 360°F.

2. Season the ½ cup rice flour with salt.

3. Dust the shrimp in the seasoned flour.

4. Combine the egg yolks and seltzer, stirring until combined. Add the 2 cups of rice flour and stir just until mixed, but not smooth.

5. Batter the shrimp, allowing the excess to drip off. In batches, fry the shrimp until golden brown, about 1–2 minutes. Drain on a paper towel–lined plate.

6. Meanwhile, whisk together the dressing ingredients in a large bowl. Add the shrimp to the bowl, toss to coat, and skewer 3 shrimp together. Transfer to a platter. Garnish generously with chives and enjoy.

Toasted Ravioli with Pecorino Fonduta

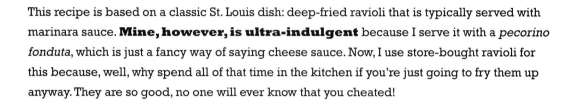

Serves: 10   Prep Time: 20 minutes   Cook Time: 20 minutes

This recipe is based on a classic St. Louis dish: deep-fried ravioli that is typically served with marinara sauce. **Mine, however, is ultra-indulgent** because I serve it with a *pecorino fonduta*, which is just a fancy way of saying cheese sauce. Now, I use store-bought ravioli for this because, well, why spend all of that time in the kitchen if you're just going to fry them up anyway. They are so good, no one will ever know that you cheated!

1 pound, store-bought, 1-inch-square ricotta ravioli, frozen

1 cup all-purpose flour

Salt and freshly ground black pepper, to taste

3 eggs, beaten

½ cup half-and-half

2 cups plain bread crumbs

1 cup Pecorino Romano, grated, plus more

2 tablespoons dried thyme

2 tablespoons dried parsley

1 lemon, zested

Extra-virgin olive oil, for frying

FOR THE PECORINO FONDUTA:

1 cup half-and-half

½ cup Pecorino Romano, grated

1 cup fontina cheese, shredded

4 egg yolks

Salt and freshly ground black pepper, to taste

FOR THE TOASTED RAVIOLI:

1. Fill a large pot with water and bring to a boil. When water is boiling, add ravioli and cook for 3 minutes. Remove and immediately submerge in ice water, then drain and place on a clean towel.

2. To dry, place 3 large bowls or baking dishes in front of you.

3. In the first one, add the flour and season with salt and pepper. In the second, whisk together the eggs and half-and-half until well combined. In the third, whisk together the bread crumbs, cheese, and herbs until well combined. Working in batches, place some of the cooked ravioli in the flour mixture. Toss to coat. Next place in the egg mixture and toss to coat.

4. Finally, place in the bread crumb mixture and toss to coat. Meanwhile, preheat a nonstick sauté pan over medium-high heat. Add a drizzle of olive oil and add the breaded ravioli. Cook until golden brown and toasted on both sides.

5. Remove to a platter.

6. Before serving, garnish the ravioli with more freshly grated lemon zest and Pecorino Romano.

7. Serve with pecorino fonduta.

FOR THE PECORINO FONDUTA:

8. In a medium saucepan over medium heat, add the half-and-half and bring to a simmer. Remove from heat and add the cheese and egg yolks, whisking constantly. Season to taste with salt and pepper.

Crunchy Chicken and Potato Chip Sandwich

Serves: 4   Prep Time: 1 hour, 15 minutes   Cook Time: 30 minutes

Carla and I paired up against our very own Michael Symon and Curtis Stone for a guilty pleasure battle of the sexes, and guess who won . . .that's right, the ladies! When we asked the judges what clinched the title for us, the answer: the chips! That's right, people, potato chips, corn chips, whatever, you can't go wrong with chips on your sandwich. So next time you pile that sandwich high, **don't forget the chips**.

FOR THE HOT FRIED CHICKEN:

1 quart water

¼ cup hot sauce

¼ cup kosher salt, for brine

¼ cup sugar

1½ pounds chicken cutlets

3 cups flour

1 teaspoon ground black pepper

¼ cup vegetable oil,
plus 3 tablespoons

1 tablespoon cayenne pepper

½ teaspoon salt, for the spiced oil

½ teaspoon paprika

¼ teaspoon garlic powder

½ teaspoon sugar

Potato buns, to serve

FOR THE SLAW:

2 cups shredded red cabbage

½ cup shredded carrot,
about 1–2 carrots

3 scallions, thinly sliced

¼ cup bread and butter pickles,
chopped

1 cup mayonnaise

2 lemons, juiced

2 garlic cloves, grated

Salt and freshly ground black
pepper, to taste

1. Whisk water, hot sauce, kosher salt, and sugar in a bowl until salt and sugar dissolve. Add chicken and refrigerate at least 1 hour.

2. In a large Dutch oven, heat ¼ cup oil to 350°F. Remove chicken from hot sauce marinade and pat dry. Arrange on a wire rack in a single layer.

3. In a medium bowl, combine the flour, salt, and pepper. oil Transfer flour to a mesh strainer and dust chicken lightly on both sides. Allow to air-dry in the refrigerator for 1 hour; keep the flour.

4. Remove chicken from the refrigerator and dust heavily with more flour, then press to help cake on the flour for extra crispiness.

5. Fry chicken in preheated oil until it reaches an internal temperature of 160°F, about 3–4 minutes. Remove to a paper towel–lined plate.

6. Heat remaining oil in small saucepan over medium heat until shimmering. Add cayenne, paprika, salt, garlic powder, and sugar. Cook until fragrant, about 30 seconds. Transfer to a small bowl and drizzle over the chicken to serve.

7. Place a schmear of spread on the bottom bun and top with chicken. Finish with coleslaw and potato chips.

FOR THE SLAW:

8. Toss together the ingredients in a large bowl until evenly dressed. Adjust seasoning to taste.

FOR THE SPREAD:

9. Mix together the ingredients until evenly combined.

FOR THE SPREAD:

¼ cup mayonnaise

1 tablespoon honey

1 teaspoon paprika

Polish Boy

Serves: 4   **Prep Time: 1 hour**   **Cook Time: 25 minutes**

This sandwich is one of my all-time favorite hometown treats. It's the king of ballpark food, and as far as guilty pleasures go, it can't be beat. There is nothing like watching the Cleveland Indians with home-field advantage while eating an enormous sausage sandwich stuffed with French fries and topped with spicy slaw and drinking an ice-cold beer. **It's a home run!** Thank you Cleveland for creating this magical dish!

FOR THE SHA SHA SAUCE:

12 hot, jarred banana peppers

4 garlic cloves

1 cup yellow mustard

1 cup white wine vinegar

¾ cup sugar

⅓ cup all-purpose flour

FOR THE SLAW:

½ head Napa cabbage

½ clove garlic, minced

½ small red onion

½ fresh jalapeño, minced

3 tablespoons champagne vinegar

1 tablespoon Dijon mustard

2 tablespoons yellow mustard

2 tablespoons mayonnaise

1 tablespoon sugar

1½ teaspoons salt

1 tablespoon Worcestershire sauce

¼ cup Sha Sha

FOR THE FRIES:

2 pounds russet potatoes

Canola oil

Salt, to taste

FOR THE SHA SHA SAUCE:

1. In a food processor, puree the peppers, garlic, mustard, and vinegar.

2. Pour the puree into a nonreactive saucepan, then add the sugar and bring it to a boil over high heat. Lower the heat and simmer the mixture for 30 minutes.

3. In a small bowl or juice glass, mix the flour and a ½ cup of water to make a smooth paste. Whisk it into the pepper mixture and continue to simmer for 20 minutes, stirring regularly, until it becomes very thick. Let the sauce cool, then pour it into a covered nonreactive container (such as a glass jar). The sauce can be refrigerated for up to 1 month.

FOR THE SLAW:

4. In a medium bowl, mix together the cabbage, garlic, onion, jalapeño, vinegar, mustards, mayonnaise, sugar, salt, Worcestershire sauce, and Sha Sha sauce. Cover and refrigerate 1 hour.

FOR THE FRIES:

5. Peel the potatoes and cut them into long fries, about a ¼-inch thick. As you cut them, put them in a bowl of cold water to cover.

6. Pour enough oil into a medium pot so that the oil comes 3 inches up the sides. Heat the oil to 275°F.

7. Drain the fries and pat dry. Working in batches, if necessary, cook them in the oil for about 5 minutes; they should be soft and pale. Remove them from the oil and turn heat to 350°F.

FOR THE SANDWICH:

4 kielbasa sausages

4 hoagie rolls

8. Add the fries in batches, if necessary, to the oil and cook, stirring gently, until the fries are golden brown, about 5 minutes. Remove them from the oil to a large paper towel–lined plate and season them with salt, shaking to distribute the seasonings evenly.

9. Fry kielbasa for 5 minutes until done. Place in a hoagie bun, top with slaw and fries, and serve.

Chicken Mac-and-Cheese Burgers

Serves: 6   Prep Time: 15 minutes   Cook Time: 20 minutes

I make chicken burgers all of the time because I want to be healthy. But when I want to be bad, I top those chicken patties with mac and cheese. That's right, I said it, and I serve them on a brioche bun. Sometimes you've just gotta **go big or pack it up and go home!**

FOR THE BURGERS:

1½ pounds ground chicken

1 zucchini, grated

1 onion, grated and excess moisture squeezed out

1 carrot, grated

¾ cup bread crumbs

1 egg

Salt and freshly ground black pepper, to taste

FOR THE MAC AND CHEESE:

1 pound macaroni

2 tablespoons butter

1 onion, diced

1 garlic clove, minced

1 teaspoon paprika

1 teaspoon dried mustard

2 tablespoons flour

2 cups milk

1 pound cheddar cheese

Salt and freshly ground black pepper, to taste

TO ASSEMBLE:

6 brioche rolls

1. In a large bowl, combine the chicken with the grated zucchini, onion, carrot, bread crumbs, egg, and a generous pinch of salt and freshly cracked pepper. Fold together until combined. With dampened hands, form into patties, and arrange on a parchment-lined sheet tray.

2. Place the patties on a lightly-oiled griddle over medium heat for 6–8 minutes or until cooked through.

3. Halve the brioche rolls and lightly toast.

TO ASSEMBLE THE BURGER:

4. Place a chicken patty on the bottom bun and top with a large scoop of mac and cheese.

FOR THE MAC AND CHEESE:

5. Cook the macaroni according to package directions in salted water. Drain.

6. In a large sauce pan, sauté the onions and garlic in the butter over medium heat until soft, about 4 minutes. Add the paprika and the mustard and season with salt and pepper. Whisk in the 2 tablespoons of flour and the milk, and stir until it starts to thicken slightly, about 4 minutes. Fold in the cheese and add the macaroni. Stir together and set aside.

The Chew: An Essential Guide to Cooking and Entertaining

Dynamite Disco Fries

Serves: 4   Prep Time: 10 minutes   Cook Time: 45 minutes

When I think of the 1970s, I think of just one thing: DISCO! Here I've combined two of my favorite things. . . disco and dining. **This dish takes me back** to when I would go out dancing all night long, and I would be starving after working up such a sweat. We would hit the twenty-four-hour diner, and I would stuff my face with this delicious dish.

FOR THE HERB FRIES:

3 pounds russet potatoes, scrubbed clean and cut into ½-inch-thick fries

Canola oil, for frying

3 tablespoons parsley, chopped

2 tablespoons rosemary, chopped

2 tablespoons thyme, chopped

Salt, to taste

Freshly cracked black pepper

FOR THE AGED CHEDDAR DIP:

2 tablespoons butter

1 shallot, minced

2 garlic cloves, minced

2 tablespoons flour

½ teaspoon cayenne pepper

2 cups milk

1 pound aged white cheddar cheese, shredded

Salt, to taste

Freshly cracked black pepper

1. Heat oil to 300°F.

2. Working in batches, fry potatoes for 6 minutes at 300°F. Remove and drain on a cooling rack over a rimmed baking sheet.

3. Increase oil temperature to 365°F.

4. Working in batches, fry the parcooked potatoes for 5–6 minutes until rich golden and crispy. Remove to a paper towel–lined plate. Immediately season with herbs, salt, and pepper.

5. Serve hot with aged cheddar dip.

FOR THE AGED CHEDDAR DIP:

6. Heat a saucepot over medium with butter. Add the shallot, season with salt, and cook until translucent, about 3 minutes. Add the garlic and cook just until fragrant.

7. Sprinkle in the flour and cayenne pepper, and stir to form a wet paste. Stir in the milk, whisking vigorously to try to avoid lumps. Season with salt and pepper. Cook for about 5–6 minutes or until slightly thickened.

8. Remove from heat and stir in the cheese, adjusting seasoning to taste. This dip can be made a few days in advance and stored in the fridge.

Toasted Pepperoni Bread with Burrata

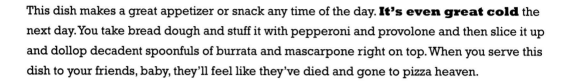

Serves: 12   Prep Time: 2 hours, 15 minutes   Cook Time: 15 minutes

This dish makes a great appetizer or snack any time of the day. **It's even great cold** the next day. You take bread dough and stuff it with pepperoni and provolone and then slice it up and dollop decadent spoonfuls of burrata and mascarpone right on top. When you serve this dish to your friends, baby, they'll feel like they've died and gone to pizza heaven.

1 pound store-bought pizza dough (or pizza dough), thawed according to package instructions

¼ pound provolone cheese, thinly sliced and roughly chopped

¼ pound Swiss cheese, thinly sliced and roughly chopped

¼ pound mozzarella cheese, shredded

2 eggs, divided, whisked

½ pound pepperoni, thinly sliced

Pinch of coarse sea salt

2 tablespoons sesame seeds

Olive oil

Melted butter

¼ pound burrata or ricotta

½ cup mascarpone

Fresh basil chiffonade, to serve

1. Place dough in a lightly oiled bowl. Drizzle a little more olive oil on top of the dough and smear all over the top. Cover the bowl with a damp towel and place in a warm area. Let the dough rise until it doubles in size.

2. Combine the cheeses and one whisked egg in a medium bowl. Set aside. Whisk the remaining egg with a splash of water for egg wash; set aside.

3. Preheat oven to 375°F.

4. Grease a 18x26-inch (or large) baking sheet with melted butter. Stretch and roll out the dough to fit inside the baking sheet. Spread the cheese mixture all over the dough. Lay the slices of pepperoni on top of the cheese mixture. Place the pan horizontally to you. Beginning with the bottom of the dough, roll up like a jelly roll. Place the roll seam-side down on the pan and fold the ends of the dough down to conceal the filling. Pinch to secure seams. Brush the top with egg wash. Sprinkle with sea salt and sesame seeds. Bake for 15–20 minutes until cooked through and golden brown on top.

5. Remove from the oven and let cool on a baking sheet. When cool enough to handle, slice the dough into ½-inch slices.

6. Preheat a griddle over medium heat. Melt some butter and place a few slices of pepperoni bread into the pan to toast. When golden brown, flip and toast the other side. Serve the toasted bread with chilled burrata or mascarpone cheese and fresh basil leaves.

Creamy Buttery Crab Dip

Serves: 10–12　　**Prep Time:** *15 minutes*　　**Cook Time:** *20 minutes*

One of my favorite guilty pleasures has to be a really creamy, buttery crab dip. This is great for any party, including my favorite kind . . . one where they serve booze. This makes a whole lot of dip, so what I like to do is bake it in two smaller baking dishes so that I can heat one up at a time (so that my guests always have hot crab dip). Either that, or I hide the second dish until after my guests leave so that I can have it all to myself.

16 ounces lump crab meat, picked through for shells

2 tablespoons melted butter

2 tablespoons flour

1 cup milk

1 cup heavy cream

½ teaspoon freshly grated nutmeg

½ teaspoon cayenne

2 egg yolks

8 ounces cream cheese

8 ounces Monterey Jack cheese, shredded

2 tablespoons chopped chives

Salt and freshly ground black pepper, to taste

1 cup buttery round crackers, plus more to serve

2 tablespoons butter, cubed

1. Preheat oven to 350°F.

2. Melt the butter in a large, heavy-bottomed pot over medium-high heat. Add the flour, stirring to combine, and cook for 2 minutes until light golden. Slowly pour in the milk and cream, whisking as you pour. Bring the liquid to a simmer, stirring the whole time. Simmer until the sauce is thick enough to cover the back of a wooden spoon. Add the nutmeg, cayenne, egg yolks, cream cheese, Monterey Jack cheese, and chives. Season to taste with salt and pepper. Stir until combined and the mixture is smooth. Fold in the crab meat. Pour the mixture into a buttered casserole dish. Crumble the crackers on top and dot with a few pieces of butter.

3. Place in the oven to bake for 15 minutes. Place under the broiler until golden brown. Serve the dip warm with more buttery crackers.

Barbecue Chicken Wing Cupcakes

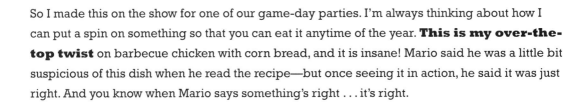

Serves: 9   Prep Time: 45 minutes   Cook Time: 50 minutes

So I made this on the show for one of our game-day parties. I'm always thinking about how I can put a spin on something so that you can eat it anytime of the year. **This is my over-the-top twist** on barbecue chicken with corn bread, and it is insane! Mario said he was a little bit suspicious of this dish when he read the recipe—but once seeing it in action, he said it was just right. And you know when Mario says something's right . . . it's right.

FOR THE MUFFINS:

2 cups cornmeal

2 tablespoons sugar

4 teaspoons baking powder

½ teaspoon salt

3 eggs

1 cup buttermilk

1 cup cream-style corn

½ cup vegetable oil, plus
3 tablespoons for skillet

FOR THE BARBECUE SAUCE:

1 cup ketchup

¼ cup white vinegar

¼ cup brown sugar

2 tablespoons butter

1 tablespoon Worcestershire
sauce

1 tablespoon lemon juice

1 teaspoon jerk chicken rub

½ teaspoon salt

¼ teaspoon cayenne pepper

FOR THE MOLASSES
BUTTERCREAM:

1 stick butter, at room
temperature

2 tablespoons molasses

¼ cup confectioners' sugar

1 teaspoon vanilla

FOR THE MUFFINS:

1. Preheat oven to 425°F.

2. In a medium bowl, combine dry ingredients. In a small bowl, combine the wet ingredients.

3. Pour the wet ingredients into the dry ingredients and mix until smooth. Spray muffin tin, and then pour the batter into it. Bake for 15–20 minutes.

FOR THE BARBECUE SAUCE:

4. Mix all barbecue sauce ingredients in a small pot and simmer over a low heat for 15–20 minutes. Adjust salt, if necessary.

FOR THE MOLASSES BUTTERCREAM:

5. In a large bowl with an electric mixer, or in the bowl of a standing mixer, cream together room temperature butter, molasses, confectioners' sugar, vanilla, salt, and cinnamon until fluffy and smooth. Set aside.

FOR THE JERK CHICKEN RUB:

6. Combine all the ingredients in a small bowl.

FOR THE WINGS:

7. Preheat a grill or grill-pan to medium-high heat. Season the wings with salt, pepper, and jerk chicken rub.

8. Lightly oil the grill or grill-pan with olive oil and arrange wings. Grill for 3–4 minutes per side, until cooked through. Transfer wings to a large bowl, and toss the wings in the barbecue sauce to cover.

Pinch of salt

Pinch of cinnamon

FOR THE JERK CHICKEN RUB:

3 tablespoons smoked paprika

2 tablespoons sweet paprika

2 tablespoons cayenne pepper

1 tablespoon onion powder

1 tablespoon garlic powder

1 teaspoon dried oregano

1 teaspoon dried thyme

1 teaspoon salt

FOR THE WINGS:

9 chicken wings

Salt and freshly ground black pepper, to taste

Olive oil

Chicken rub (above)

TO ASSEMBLE:

9. Glaze each of the muffins with the molasses butter and set aside. Once it has set, top with a chicken wing to serve.

CLINTON'S "IT'S THE LITTLE THINGS" TIP

When I'm entertaining and I know that I'm going to be serving a really messy dish like Barbecue Chicken Wing Cupcakes, I always make these warm towelettes for my guests to use to clean their hands. I just take a little bit of baby wash and add it to a bowl with a couple of drops of lavender essential oil and some warm water. Then I dip the towels in the water, roll them up, and place them on a tray for my guests. If you want, you can even warm them in the microwave for 20 seconds right before your guests arrive. It's the little things that make a party great.

Clinton's General Tso's Chicken

Serves: 4   Prep Time: 15 minutes   Cook Time: 7–10 minutes

I've said it before and I'll say it again: my go-to guilty pleasure is Chinese takeout. Specifically, General Tso's chicken. **I love everything about it**—except for the calories. So I came up with a recipe that is slightly better for me so that I can eat it lying down on the couch, watching *America's Next Top Model*, whenever I want.

FOR THE SAUCE:

1 tablespoon cornstarch

½ cup cold water

4 garlic cloves, sliced

2 teaspoons fresh ginger, grated

3 tablespoons honey

2 tablespoons low-sodium soy sauce

2 tablespoons Chinese rice wine

1 tablespoon red pepper flakes

1 pound broccoli florets

FOR THE CHICKEN:

3 tablespoons cornstarch

1 pound boneless, skinless chicken breasts, cut into 1-inch pieces

½ teaspoon salt

¼ teaspoon pepper

2 tablespoons vegetable oil

FOR THE SIDE DISH:

1½ cups white rice

FOR THE GARNISH:

4 scallions, thinly sliced greens only

1 teaspoon sesame seeds

1. Bring a pot of water to a boil and season with salt. Add broccoli and cook for 2–3 minutes until bright green. Place in an ice bath to cool. Remove and pat dry.

2. Begin making the sauce in a large bowl by mixing together 1 tablespoon cornstarch and ½ cup of cold water until smooth. Add garlic, ginger, honey, soy sauce, Chinese rice wine, and red pepper flakes. Set aside.

3. In a separate bowl, mix cornstarch, salt, and pepper together until combined. Add chicken and blanched broccoli and toss to coat.

4. Cook rice according to package instructions.

5. Heat a large nonstick skillet with vegetable oil. Shake excess coating off the chicken and broccoli and cook in batches until golden, 4–6 minutes. Add the sauce mixture and cook until the sauce has thickened. Plate with rice. Add scallions and sesame seeds for garnish.

Meat Loaf with Creamy Shells 'n' Peas

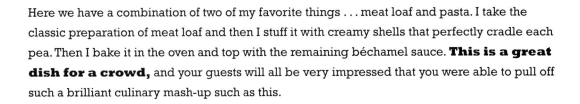

Serves: 12   **Prep Time:** 30 minutes   **Cook Time:** 1 hour

Here we have a combination of two of my favorite things . . . meat loaf and pasta. I take the classic preparation of meat loaf and then I stuff it with creamy shells that perfectly cradle each pea. Then I bake it in the oven and top with the remaining béchamel sauce. **This is a great dish for a crowd,** and your guests will all be very impressed that you were able to pull off such a brilliant culinary mash-up such as this.

FOR THE MEAT LOAF:

2 tablespoons olive oil

1 yellow onion, chopped

2 cloves garlic, minced

2 pounds sweet Italian pork sausage, removed from casings

2 pounds lean ground beef

4 cups plain bread crumbs

1 cup freshly grated Pecorino Romano

3 eggs, lightly beaten

1 cup whole milk

1 cup tomato puree, divided

½ cup parsley, chopped

2 tablespoons brown sugar

2 tablespoons white vinegar

Salt and freshly ground black pepper, to taste

FOR THE FILLING:

½ pound small shell-shaped pasta

Mario's béchamel sauce

1 cup freshly grated Parmesan

8 ounces frozen peas, thawed

Salt and freshly ground black pepper, to taste

1. Preheat oven to 375°F.

2. In a small sauté pan, preheat a couple tablespoons of olive oil over medium heat. Add the onion and garlic, then season with salt and pepper and sauté for 5 minutes until translucent. Set aside to cool.

3. In a large bowl, combine the sausage, ground beef, cooled onion and garlic mixture, bread crumbs, Pecorino Romano, eggs, whole milk, a ½ cup of tomato puree, and parsley. Season with a generous pinch of salt and freshly ground black pepper to taste. Using your fingertips, bring together the ingredients until just combined.

4. Meanwhile, prepare Mario's béchamel sauce. Add the Parmesan to the béchamel sauce.

5. Bring a large pot of salted water to a boil. Drop the pasta and cook until al dente. Drain and set aside. Dress the pasta with half of the béchamel sauce and add the peas. Season to taste with salt.

6. Line a baking sheet with parchment paper. Place ¾ of the meat loaf mixture, lengthwise, down the center of the prepared pan The loaf should be about 5–6 inches widthwise. Using your hands, create a well, lengthwise, down the center of the loaf. Leave high edges along the sides and the ends of the loaf. Pour the creamy shells and peas mixture into the well of the meat loaf. Enclose the creamy shells and peas mixture by pushing the edges together and using the remaining meat loaf mixture to enclose the top. Press the meat mixture to tightly secure the exposed filling.

7. In a small bowl, stir to combine the remaining tomato puree, brown sugar, and vinegar. Season with salt to taste. Brush the tomato mixture over the top of the meat loaf. Sprinkle the top of the loaf with some freshly ground black pepper.

FOR THE BÉCHAMEL SAUCE:

5 tablespoons unsalted butter

¼ cup flour

3 cups whole milk

2 teaspoons kosher salt

½ teaspoon freshly grated nutmeg

8. Place the loaf in the oven to bake for 1 hour and 15 minutes.

9. Let the meat loaf rest for 10 to 15 minutes before slicing and serving. Drizzle the sliced meat loaf with leftover béchamel sauce. (Tip: Do not overwork your mixture to avoid a tough meat loaf.)

FOR THE BÉCHAMEL SAUCE:

10. In a medium saucepan, melt the butter over medium heat. Add the flour and stir until smooth. Cook until light golden brown, about 5 minutes. Add the milk, 1 cup at a time, whisking continuously until smooth. Bring to a boil and cook for 5 minutes. Season with salt and nutmeg and set aside.

Burger Bread Pudding

Serves: 6   Prep Time: 25 minutes   Cook Time: 30 minutes

There is no doubt in my mind that one of the best foods ever created in the history of the world is the beloved cheeseburger. **I can't get enough of them.** So here I have created a version of a bacon-cheeseburger that you can serve at your next brunch. It's got everything you want in a burger: bacon, cheese, potato rolls, all baked up in one beautiful casserole. It's even topped with pickles. What more could you ask for?

4 potato buns, torn into pieces or large dice

½ pound thick-sliced bacon, medium dice

1 pound ground beef

1½ cups red onion, medium dice

2½ cups sharp cheddar, grated

6 large eggs

2 cups whole milk

Salt and freshly ground black pepper, to taste

½ cup pickles, to garnish

1. Preheat the oven to 375°F. Spray a 13x9-inch baking dish with cooking spray.

2. Place torn bread on a sheet pan in an even layer. Drizzle with olive oil and toss to coat. Toast for 15 minutes until golden brown. Remove from the oven and place torn bread into a large mixing bowl. Set aside.

3. In the meantime, in a large sauté pan over medium-high heat, add bacon. Cook until crispy, stirring occasionally, about 5 minutes. Remove to a paper towel–lined plate and set aside.

4. To the same pan, add the ground beef. Cook, breaking up the meat with the back of a spoon, about 5 minutes, or until meat is browned.

5. Add the red onion and cook an additional 3 minutes, until the onions begin to soften. Pour the meat mixture over the toasted bread. Toss to combine.

6. Add half of the bread and meat mixture to the prepared pan. Sprinkle 1½ cups of shredded cheese evenly over the top. Add the other half of the bread and meat mixture to the top. Top with remaining 1 cup of shredded cheese.

7. In a large bowl, whisk together eggs and milk. Season with salt and pepper. Pour the custard over the bread and gently press down. (At this point, you may wrap the dish tightly in plastic and refrigerate overnight.)

8. Bake, uncovered, for 30–35 minutes until golden brown. Remove from the oven and allow to set for 10 minutes for serving. Garnish with pickles on top.

Daphne's "Alfredo"

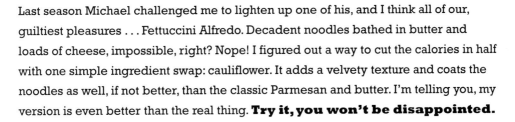

Serves: 4   Prep Time: 10 minutes   Cook Time: 45 minutes

Last season Michael challenged me to lighten up one of his, and I think all of our, guiltiest pleasures . . . Fettuccini Alfredo. Decadent noodles bathed in butter and loads of cheese, impossible, right? Nope! I figured out a way to cut the calories in half with one simple ingredient swap: cauliflower. It adds a velvety texture and coats the noodles as well, if not better, than the classic Parmesan and butter. I'm telling you, my version is even better than the real thing. **Try it, you won't be disappointed.**

4 cups cauliflower, cut into large chunks

1 cup milk

2 tablespoons butter

1 pound fettuccine

1 large shallot, finely minced

½ cup white wine

¼ teaspoon nutmeg, freshly grated

¼ cup Parmesan, freshly grated

⅓ cup parsley, chopped

Olive oil

Salt and freshly ground black pepper, to taste

1. Place the milk and the cauliflower in a large saucepot and season with salt and pepper. Bring to a boil, reduce to a simmer, cover, and cook until fork tender, about 8–10 minutes.

2. Using a slotted utensil, transfer the cauliflower to a blender. Add the milk and butter and puree until smooth. Season with salt and pepper.

3. Bring a large pot of salted water to a boil.

4. Cook the pasta 1 minute less than the package instructions.

5. While the pasta is cooking, place a large sauté pan over medium heat and add 1–2 tablespoons of olive oil. Add the shallot, season with salt, and cook for 2–3 minutes, or until slightly tender.

6. Deglaze with the white wine and allow to reduce by half, about 1–2 minutes.

7. Add the cauliflower puree and loosen the sauce with about ⅓ of a cup of pasta water.

8. Remove the pasta from the water and add it to the cauliflower puree. Grate fresh nutmeg over the top.

9. Toss again and add more cooking water if the pasta seems too dry.

10. Add the Parmesan and parsley and toss to coat.

The CHEW

TAILGATE
GREATS

Pineapple Upside Down Monkey Bread

Serves: 12   Prep Time: 5 minutes   Cook Time: 1 hour

There is nothing better than a **sticky, gooey, pull-apart monkey bread,** except maybe one that's topped with pineapples and maraschino cherries. The beauty of this dish is that you make it with canned biscuits. That's right, people, let the store do the work for you!

2 cans (16 ounces each) refrigerated biscuit dough

½ cup sweetened shredded coconut

2 tablespoons sugar

½ cup butter

⅔ cup brown sugar

1 cup maraschino cherries, halved

3 cups fresh pineapple, diced

1. Preheat oven to 350°F. Prepare a fluted tube pan by spraying it with nonstick baking spray.

2. Cut each biscuit into 6 pieces and place in a large mixing bowl. Sprinkle the biscuits with the shredded coconut and sugar and toss to coat. Set aside.

3. In a nonstick sauté pan over medium-low heat, melt the butter. Add the brown sugar and stir until the sugar has dissolved. Pour the mixture evenly into the bottom of the tube pan. Distribute the cherries on top of the melted sugar mixture, then add the cubed pineapple. Top with the sugar-coconut coated biscuits. Place in the oven and bake for 45–50 minutes, or until golden brown. Remove from the oven and allow to cool for 5 minutes. Using a cake stand or platter, invert the monkey bread.

4. Serve warm.

MARIO'S "DON'T WASTE IT" TIP

Don't throw away that pineapple core! You can use it in marinades to tenderize big pieces of beef or pork. Daphne even puts the core right into her smoothies in the morning because it's super good for you.

Bourbon, Bacon Caramel Banana Split

Serves: 5   Prep Time: 5 minutes   Cook Time: 15 minutes

Bourbon, bacon, bananas—oh, my! This flavor combination is something that I truly cannot resist. I love the way the hot caramel sauce just slightly melts the ice cream so that the banana just floats in a pool of deliciousness; and, of course, you know I love the salty addition of bacon to amp things up.

FOR THE BACON CARAMEL:

1 cup bacon, diced

3 tablespoons brown sugar

2 tablespoons bourbon

3–4 teaspoons heavy cream

FOR THE WHIPPED CREAM:

1 cup heavy cream

2 tablespoons sugar

1 teaspoon vanilla extract

FOR THE BANANA SPLIT:

5 whole bananas

Bacon caramel sauce

Whipped cream

5 good quality maraschino cherries

Shaved chocolate

1. Heat a medium sauté pan over medium heat and add the bacon. Cook the bacon until crunchy, about 6 minutes. Once crispy, pour off the excess fat and add the brown sugar, then stir to dissolve. Deglaze with the bourbon and add the heavy cream. Heat through and keep warm while you make the whipped cream.

2. Add the cup of heavy cream to a large bowl and whisk in the sugar and vanilla. Whisk until soft peaks form, about 5 minutes. Set aside while you assemble the banana split.

3. Cut a banana in half lengthwise and place it on a platter. Top with the bacon caramel, whipped cream, maraschino cherries, and shaved chocolate. Repeat with the remaining bananas.

S'Mores Cream Puffs

Serves: 12   Prep Time: 20 minutes   Cook Time: 55 minutes

Everyone's childhood guilty pleasure is a s'more! Am I right? Well I've taken that kiddie treat to a whole new level with my S'Mores Cream Puffs. It's basically a cream-filled doughnut with toasted marshmallows on top, dipped in chocolate, and sprinkled with graham crackers. It's huge, it's delicious, and boy, is it messy! **All the goodness you remember as a kid** but decadent enough to satisfy the adult in you.

FOR THE PUFFS:

1 cup unsalted butter

2 cups water

Pinch of salt

2 cups unbleached flour

7 eggs

FOR THE CREAM FILLING:

2 cups whole milk

5 large egg yolks

1 cup sugar

¼ cup cornstarch

1 teaspoon vanilla extract

FOR THE GANACHE:

½ cup unsalted butter, room temperature, cut into tablespoon-size pieces

8 ounces semisweet chocolate chips

FOR THE TOPPINGS:

Crushed graham crackers

Mini-marshmallows

FOR THE PUFFS:

1. Preheat oven to 400°F. Line sheet pans with parchment and lightly coat with cooking spray.

2. In a medium pot, bring butter, water, and salt to a boil. Add all the flour at once, turning heat down to medium-low and begin to beat until mixture pulls away from sides and forms a ball.

3. Transfer to the bowl of a standing mixer and beat at medium speed until cooled slightly. Turn speed up to high and add the eggs, one at a time, until fully incorporated. Do not add the next egg until the current egg is fully incorporated.

4. When dough comes together, after around 10 minutes, transfer to piping bag. Pipe 3-inch rounds onto the parchment-lined sheet pan, leaving space between each.

5. Bake for about 40 minutes until outsides are golden brown and the insides of the puffs sound hollow. Cool completely before filling.

FOR THE CREAM FILLING:

6. In a medium saucepan, whisk together milk, egg yolks, sugar, and cornstarch. Place over low heat, whisking gently just until the mixture bubbles, about 15 minutes. Immediately remove from the heat. Strain through a fine-mesh sieve into a large bowl. Stir in the vanilla extract. Press plastic wrap directly on the top of the cream and place in fridge to cool completely, approximately 2 hours.

7. To fill the puffs, transfer the pastry cream to a piping bag, with a medium tip. Use the tip to break a small hole in the puff, and fill.

FOR THE GANACHE:

8. Heat chocolate in a double boiler. Add the room temperature butter, a piece at a time, melting into the chocolate. Dip puffs into the mixture.

9. Top with crushed graham crackers and mini-marshmallows. Allow to dry on a parchment-lined sheet pan.

Daphne's Baked Doughnuts and Coconut Cream

Who doesn't love a delicious doughnut? I developed these little guys because I love doughnuts so much that I have a really hard time eating just one. Now with these minis, I can have three or four for the amount of calories of one big doughnut! How great is that?

DRY INGREDIENTS:

1 cup all-purpose flour

½ cup sugar

1½ teaspoons baking powder

¼ teaspoon salt

⅛ teaspoon nutmeg

Pinch of cinnamon

WET INGREDIENTS:

½ cup nonfat yogurt

½ teaspoon apple-cider vinegar

½ teaspoon vanilla extract

2 egg whites

3 tablespoons coconut oil

FOR THE COCONUT MILK WHIPPED CREAM:

¾ cup coconut cream from 10-ounce can of coconut milk (refrigerate to help separation)

¼ cup sugar

½ teaspoon vanilla extract

Pinch of salt

Dark chocolate, melted, for drizzling (optional)

1. Preheat oven to 350°F. Grease a mini-doughnut pan with vegetable spray.

2. In a large bowl, combine dry ingredients with a whisk to mix thoroughly. Combine wet ingredients in a small saucepan over medium-low heat and mix. This mixture should not get too hot. It should feel slightly warm. It should take approximately 2 minutes.

3. Add wet ingredients to dry ingredients and mix until just combined. It should form a very soft dough.

4. Fill piping bag or zip-top bag with batter. Cut off the tip and pipe about 1 tablespoon of batter into each mini-doughnut mold.

5. Bake for 12–15 minutes. They should not be browned on top. A cake tester should come out clean. Invert the hot pan over a cutting board or cooling rack to release the doughnuts. Allow to cool completely.

6. Cut doughnuts in half lengthwise and spread with coconut cream.

FOR THE COCONUT MILK WHIPPED CREAM:

7. Chill a mixing bowl and beaters in the freezer for at least 20 minutes.

8. Using a spoon, skim the top layer of cream from a 10-ounce can of coconut milk (about ¾ cup of cream) and place it in the chilled mixing bowl with sugar, vanilla, and a pinch of salt. Beat on low speed until small bubbles form, about 30 seconds. Increase the speed to high and continue beating until the cream thickens and light peaks form, about 2 minutes.

9. Serve immediately or cover and refrigerate for up to 4 hours.

10. Drizzle dark chocolate over finished doughnuts (optional).

HOW TO BRINE LIKE A BATALI

In my opinion there is only one way to guarantee a moist and delicious turkey come thanksgiving and that's to brine it. Brining not only keeps your turkey from drying out while cooking, it also adds tons of flavor to your bird. So if you want to score points with your new in-laws or even your 85-year-old grandma, it's all about the brine baby! —MARIO BATALI

1.

In a large stock pot combine the following:

1 gallon water

1 cup salt

2 cups maple syrup

1 head garlic, split

1 bunch rosemary, sage and thyme

Bring to a boil and then let cool to room temperature.

2.

Transfer the cooled brine to a large bucket or storage container and add the following:

1 gallon ice water

2 cups apple cider

3.

Add the turkey (12–15 lbs.)

Refrigerate overnight, but no longer than 12 hours.

VIEWER Q&A

with MARIO BATALI

• •

What's the most romantic meal you've ever made for your significant other? —Jennifer R. Berryman, Cambellsville, KY

My wife doesn't like very complicated food, nor does she enjoy multicourse meals, so for us, it's that meal that allows us to just talk, for hours, in our most honest voices. That meal is almost always roasted chicken with vegetables and a frisée salad served with that just-right glass of rosé.

What is your worst cooking mistake?
—Lara Bartels, Brenham, TX

My worst mistakes have always been inviting the wrong guest, you know the one that drinks too much or acts inappropriately. The one that won't leave at the end of the night. When it comes to the kitchen, I say there are no mistakes, just detours that force you to recalculate your course. If I've overcooked my chicken stew, believe me, before my guests arrive, I've shredded the chicken and turned them into cannelloni or enchiladas. There is no mistake so insurmountable that I have to walk up to my guests and say, "Sorry, guys, we're ordering takeout."

What is the one question that you most hate getting asked?
—Victoria Majoros, Wyckoff, NJ

"What is your death row meal?" I get asked that all the time, and honestly, I wouldn't have a death row meal. If I had to have one last meal before my execution . . . it would be a boat ride all around the world, eating the most delicious seafood, made by the best chef in each port, served with the best wine in that region. It would take me at least fifteen years to eat that meal. At that rate, I'd outlive my executioner!

When did you start wearing orange Crocs and why?
—Sharon Woody, Bronx, NY

My wife gave them to me as a gift when I opened my first restaurant, Po, because she thought that my orange high-tops would get too dirty on the line—and she was right! My first pair were orange doctor's clogs from Italy. They were supercomfortable, so comfy in fact [that] I've been wearing them ever since.

INDEX

Daphne Oz's Lunch Box Yogurt Parfait, recipe on page 116.